PATHS
to
ANSWERED
prayer

PATHS
to
ANSWERED
prayer

Trusting God's Heart
When You Don't Understand *His Plan*

HEIDI FULLER

AMBASSADOR INTERNATIONAL
GREENVILLE, SOUTH CAROLINA & BELFAST, NORTHERN IRELAND
www.ambassador-international.com
Celebrating Forty Years of Getting the Word Around

Paths to Answered Prayer

Trusting God's Heart When You Don't Understand His Plan

ISBN: 978-1-62020-869-4
eISBN: 978-1-62020-890-8

Cover Design and Page Layout by Hannah Nichols
eBook Conversion by Anna Riebe Raats
Edited by Katie Cruice Smith
Cover Photo: Rob Fuller

AMBASSADOR INTERNATIONAL
Emerald House
411 University Ridge, Suite B14
Greenville, SC 29601, USA
www.ambassador-international.com

AMBASSADOR BOOKS
The Mount
2 Woodstock Link
Belfast, BT6 8DD, Northern Ireland, UK
www.ambassadormedia.co.uk

The colophon is a trademark of Ambassador, a Christian publishing company.

Dedicated to my five precious children—Griffen, Rhys, Taerik, Drake, and Keira. They are the physical representation of a compassionate God. They are the daily reminders of His eternally good plans. They are the visible proof that He hears and mightily answers prayer.

CONTENTS

PREFACE

"Only take care, and keep your soul diligently, lest you forget the things that your eyes have seen, and lest they depart from your heart all the days of your life. Make them known to your children and your children's children" (Deut. 4:9).

PLAIN AND SIMPLE, DEUTERONOMY 4:9 was my primary motivation for writing this book. Its command to remember initiated a searching of my soul for the faithful workings of God in my life. The admonition toward diligence spurred me on through the countless hours that were poured into this monumental endeavor. The warning to preserve such memories prompted the vulnerable bearing of my soul in this spiritual diary. And from its inception, my children have always been the intended audience.

You see, after more than twenty surgeries to repair detached retinas and other resulting complications, my eyes should be blinded. Instead, they have seen many things which should be remembered. They have seen the Prince of Peace amid the darkest trials. They have seen the Wonderful Counselor amid the greatest confusion. And they have seen the Mighty God amid the strongest impossibility.

These landmark moments in my life have driven me to my knees time and time again. Such seasons of intense prayer and pleading have been followed by seasons of tremendous spiritual growth and maturity. I have witnessed the miraculous and experienced the Divine in response to my pleadings before the throne of God. Such answers to my prayers have been mountaintop experiences of overwhelming joy and worship. And I have purposed to pass on those reminders of God's power and might to my children.

Yet, throughout my sanctification journey, I have also seen my prayers answered in other ways. As I have bowed humbly before my Maker, I have learned that not all prayers were intended to be met with the miraculous. Sometimes, my supplications have led to sorrow. Sometimes, my pleas have led to pain. Sometimes, my petitions have led to heartache.

Such varied answers to my appeals have prompted me to understand more deeply God's ultimate purpose for prayer. As I have studied the Scriptures, my vision has been enlightened, and my mind has been expanded. I have learned that prayer was never created as a means to my earthly happiness. It was never intended to merely reduce my discomforts. And it was never meant as a path to ease my pain.

Prayer is the very communion of my soul with God. It is the process by which I draw near to Him and bow humbly before His throne. By prayer, I receive "power through his Spirit in [my] inner being." I gain understanding of the depths of the "love of Christ." And I realize the excellence and perfection of Almighty God (Eph. 3:14-19).

A proper prayer life takes time to grow and develop. In Luke 11:1, we hear Jesus' closest disciples ask, "Lord, teach us to pray . . . " Likewise, every believer today should request the same thing. We must recognize its vital role and embrace its magnificent power.

My personal prayer life continues to be a journey. Over the years, I have noted its development past the simple requests of a child. I witness a growing trust in a Sovereign, Heavenly Father, Who is working all things together for my good. I recognize prayer's power to mature and change me. And I meditate on the promises of my loving Lord—the promise that He is always listening (Psa. 116:1); the promise that prayer is powerful to banish burdens and pacify pressures (Phil. 4:6-7); and the promise that prayer is always met with mercy and that grace is freely given (Heb. 4:16).

My five children have inspired every letter of this book. You see, each one of them was a direct answer to my prayers. God heard my groaning as I traveled the long, lonely road of infertility. He witnessed my grief as I wept my goodbyes to eighteen babies through various adoption failures and miscarriages. He endured my anger and patiently listened to my accusations. He loved me at my lowest, and despite my unworthiness, He blessed me beyond measure.

And now, I greatly desire to share these lessons with my five treasured gifts and to inspire them to trust more deeply in the same God Who has proven to be so very faithful to me. I desire to point them toward their Creator. I desire that the footsteps of my path would make a personal relationship with Jesus Christ appear attractive to them. I desire that their hearts would see the brilliance of the Savior and recognize the power that is available because of His cross. And I desire that this chronological journey through my life would be an inspiration as they travel their own paths to answered prayer.

"I love the Lord, because he has heard my voice and my pleas for mercy.
Because he inclined his ear to me, therefore I will call on him as long as I live"
(Psa. 116:1-2).

CHAPTER ONE

SOMETIMES GOD GIVES ME EXACTLY WHAT I WANT

"Ask, and it will be given to you; seek, and you will find; knock, and it will be opened to you; If you then, who are evil, know how to give good gifts to your children, how much more will your Father who is in heaven give good gifts to those who ask him" (Matt. 7:7, 11).

IT WAS EARLY ONE SUNDAY morning in my hometown of Minneapolis, Minnesota. I was a young girl, about three years old. Our family of four was all decked out in our Sunday-best attire as we pulled into the church parking lot. Since my dad served on staff as the children's pastor of Fourth Baptist Church in the heart of downtown Minneapolis, we were typically some of the first people to arrive each Sunday. My dark blonde curls bounced up and down as I happily pranced across the pavement and toward the front door of the church building. I was especially excited this particular morning because I had been given some money—just a few simple coins to put in the offering plate during Sunday school. I proudly placed them inside my purse, which was loaded full of goodies. But somewhere between the car and the church foyer, I lost a single coin. As a young child who felt that a great treasure had suddenly vanished, I was devastated.

As we entered the church foyer, the tears flowed as I sadly explained my despair to my daddy. And while he likely had many responsibilities to prepare for that day, he paused his busy morning routine and compassionately said, "Heidi, let's pray about it." So, hand in hand, we sat there together on a bench near the entryway and prayed that God would help me to find my lost coin. However it happened, somewhere between, "Dear Jesus, I lost my offering money," and, "Amen," a single coin appeared in my dad's hand. And in those few brief moments, it was impressed upon my young heart that prayer really works!

I was once asked the question, "If you could change anything about your childhood, what would it be?" All my girlfriends involved in the discussion quickly and easily came up with an answer of some sort. However, as I sat there, nothing appeared in my mind. Certainly nothing of significance. Only in my adult life have I realized just how truly blessed my childhood really was.

Born in 1981, I was welcomed into this world by two loving parents. My dad worked hard as an assistant pastor and Christian school administrator. He was a strong, godly leader, who wisely and authoritatively guided our family. He loved surprises and was famous for booking weekend getaways that we knew nothing about. On several occasions in which we thought we were just going out for a fun family night somewhere in town, he actually drove us to the airport, opened the trunk of the car to reveal our packed luggage, then guided us toward our flights to Disneyland. Just as special as these larger excursions were our ever-faithful, Sunday morning, daddy-and-daughter donut dates.

My mom desired nothing more than a home and children. After several years of infertility, I was the answer to her many prayers. My sister, Heather, joined our family only thirteen short months after my arrival, and with that, our little family of four was completed. My mom's gift for interior design left our home looking like something from a magazine. Her skills in sewing and fashion made my sister and me some of the best dressed kids around. And as a talented musician, she poured hours of her life into teaching us both piano and vocal skills. Yes, our home was well-manicured, orderly, and full of joy. And my childhood was very blessed.

But while there were many fun trips, nice clothes, fancy restaurants, and private schools, what characterized my childhood above all else was its intense focus on God. Every single morning, I awoke to find my dad reading his Bible and praying at the kitchen table. In the evenings, he led family devotions and prayer. And every time the church doors were open, we were all there—every service, every conference, every ministry.

My parents also possessed a deep love for others. Many wonderful memories were made during monthly, small group Bible studies held in our home. We made regular visits to a local nursing home, where our family shared music with the residents as they ate their evening meal. And there were a number of times that I listened to church members give public testimony of how God miraculously provided for some financial need in their life, and I knew in my heart that my parents were the secret agents of such grace.

But above all other spiritual disciplines, prayer was highlighted. Whenever we sat down to eat a meal, we prayed. Whenever we got in the car, we prayed. Whenever we needed guidance, we prayed. Whenever we sought help or healing, we prayed. Such dependence upon God was paramount, and His ability to meet every need of man was impressed upon my mind.

At the age of five, I accepted Jesus Christ as my personal Lord and Savior. It was late one Sunday evening, and we had just returned home from church. After a series of questions about the evening message, it was there in our yellow house in downtown Minneapolis that I knelt by our gold couch with my mom and dad on either side of me. It was there that I understood that my parents' commitment to God would not save me. It was there that I realized I was a sinner who needed to be saved from the eternal punishment for my sins. It was there on that green shag carpet that I prayed a prayer of repentance and accepted the free gift of salvation through the blood of Jesus Christ. It was there that my spiritual journey of sanctification began.

I learned that I was now a child of God and that my life belonged to my Heavenly Father. I heard of His infinite love for me—a love so deep that He sacrificed His only Son to die in my place (Jn. 3:16). I grew to understand His compassion and even pity for my frailty (Psa. 103:13-14). And I developed the belief that this kind, Heavenly Being actively listened to and answered my prayers (Lk. 18). All these facets of God's nature were reasonably simple for me to grasp. With a real-life example of an earthly father who loved, sacrificed, cherished, and blessed, it was relatively easy to transfer such attributes to a good and loving Heavenly Father Who also did the same.

I was encouraged early on in my life to pray about everything. *Everything.* The big things and the small. Fervent and specific prayers were modeled before me and soon embraced personally. I heard that God was interested in every part of my life, and so every part was worth praying about. I was reminded that just as my earthly father gave me good gifts, so also my Heavenly Father desired to "give good things to those who ask him" (Matt. 7:11). I learned to pray anywhere, at any time, about anything.

As the years of my childhood passed, the needs in my life grew. They grew from my lost offering money in preschool to boy problems in junior high. By this time in my life, our family had relocated to Tempe, Arizona. Though this new desert landscape was drastically different from the cold, northern tundra of Minnesota, I quickly learned to love my new life there. In fact, the six years that our family lived in the South (1990–1996) were likely the best of my entire childhood.

My parents were both on staff at Tri-City Baptist Church and School—another large and thriving ministry. My sister and I were privileged to be part of this high-quality, Christ-centered environment. I thrived in this desert setting and excelled in all areas—academically, socially, and spiritually. The foundational principles of prayer upon which my home life had been built were now equally stressed in my church and school, as well. And by the time that I had reached the mature age of thirteen, boys were definitely at the top of my prayer list.

During the hot summer months, my sister, Heather, and I were enrolled in a special church-led enrichment program during the week, while our parents both worked. There were daily chapel services and educational outlets. There were regular excursions to the wave pool, the ice arena, and the bowling alley. But best of all, our friends were there, and we loved maintaining those relationships throughout the summer months of vacation from school.

Plus, there was this boy named Ben. He was about a year older than me—which, at age thirteen, was a big deal. Ben had his group of friends, and I had mine. Ben hardly even knew that I existed on this planet, but I very much knew that Ben existed! I was madly in love (at least for that particular season of my life). And I was desperate for Ben to notice me.

One particular Friday during this daily summer camp, a trip to Castles-n-Coasters Amusement Park was scheduled. I thought that such an exciting venue would be the perfect place for romance and wishfully dreamed that this would be the day that my connection with Ben was finally made. Because I had long been taught that God cared about all things that mattered to me, I prayed about Ben. In fact, the night before this big field trip arrived, I went into our guest room and locked the door behind me. I then went the extra spiritual step of going into the closet and shutting that door behind me as well (Matt. 6:6). There, in the darkness of that small space, I prayed. And I prayed. And I prayed. I laid everything before God—my feelings toward Ben and my desires to be noticed by him. I expressed my hopes and dreams. I requested that God's care would be tangibly demonstrated in this seemingly insignificant area of my life. I had heard various sermons in church about praying specifically to God. And so, wanting very much to see a measurable answer to my prayers, I asked God to allow Ben to ride with me on one roller coaster the next day.

I awoke that Friday morning with much excitement—both for the fun-filled excursion and for the opportunity to see what God would do as a result of my prayers. The day started much like any other. I arrived at the day camp and headed straight for my group of girlfriends. We sat on the bus and giggled the whole way there. We snapped pictures and talked nonstop. At the amusement park, we eagerly ran from ride to ride, letting out high-pitched, junior high girl squeals with each new thrill. And while I very much enjoyed each new gravity-defying adventure, I also very much watched eagerly for Ben. But the afternoon wore on without any sign of him at all.

It was about the final hour before our departure, and my friends and I scurried between rides we hoped to repeat. We stood anxiously together in the line of yet another thrilling roller coaster. After many minutes, we finally arrived at the front and were asked to step forward by groups of two and take our seats. But as our group paired off, we suddenly realized that we had an uneven number of girls. And so, I volunteered to sit alone on this one. I slowly stepped forward and took my single seat.

As I fastened my safety belt across my lap, it happened. Everything started going in slow motion—just like you would see in the most romantic of movies. As I sat there alone with one empty seat beside me, I turned my head just in time to see Ben. Walking toward me. Through a dense fog. With a bouquet of roses. OK, so maybe there was no slow motion . . . or fog . . . or roses. But there was Ben! As the park attendant announced over his loud speaker that a single seat was still available, Ben came and took that seat—next to me! He talked to me! He laughed during the ride! He smiled as the coaster camera snapped our picture together (a picture I promptly purchased afterward). And while my relationship with Ben never moved past that five-minute roller coaster ride, I went to bed that night a *very* happy girl. God answered my prayer and renewed my confidence that He, indeed, cared about every aspect of my life!

* * *

Dear child, **God answers prayer!!!** James 4:2b says, "You do not have, because you do not ask." In Matthew 7:7-8, Jesus says, "Ask, and it will be given to you; seek, and you will find; knock, and it will be opened to you. For everyone who asks receives, and the one who seeks finds, and to the one who knocks it will be opened." And in John 14:13-14, Jesus instructs Philip, "Whatever you ask in my name, this I will do, that the Father may be glorified in the Son. If you ask me anything in my name, I will do it."

One part of prayer's design is a means of obtaining those things that we desire. As we come in faith before our Creator God and humbly lay our requests at His feet, we receive the opportunity to see Him work mightily. And sometimes when we pray, God gives us exactly what we ask.

Consider Elijah for a moment. Remember how he stood alone on the top of Mount Carmel against the 450 prophets of Baal (1 Kings 18)? Despite humanly impossible odds, he courageously sought to prove to the crowds that Yahweh was the one, true God. Two altars were built, and two bulls were killed. Two sides prayed for fire from Heaven to come down and consume their sacrifices. Two sides waited.

It had long been believed that Baal was the god of fertility, who sent the rain and fire (lightning) from Heaven. This very mountain upon which they stood was thought to be his sacred dwelling place. This region near the Mediterranean Sea saw rain and lightning regularly. The prophets of Baal were given first choice of which bull they wanted. And yet, despite having every advantage, nothing happened. Baal failed to respond to their hours of fervent prayer.

When it became obvious to all that Baal refused to answer, attention was turned to Elijah. Though already the underdog, he took extra steps to remove any thought of a natural phenomenon and ordered that twelve large jars of water be poured on his altar. This completely soaked his sacrifice and flooded the trench around the base. Then, without any theatrics, Elijah prayed, "O LORD, God of Abraham, Isaac, and Israel, let it be known this day that you are God in Israel, and that I am your servant . . . " (1 Kings 18:36). Instantly, fire fell from Heaven and consumed his sacrifice. In a tremendous show of miraculous power, God answered Elijah's prayer.

Throughout the Old Testament, many similar accounts of answered prayer are recorded. In response to the very specific petition of Eliezer, God directed Rebekah to the well and prompted her to offer water to his camels (Gen. 24). After battling infertility for nineteen years, Isaac prayed for a child, and Rebekah miraculously conceived a double blessing—twin boys (Gen. 25:19-28). When Joshua needed additional daylight in his fight against the Amorites, God supernaturally slowed the sun in its orbit and extended daylight by about twenty-four hours (Josh. 10:1-15). The withered hand of King Jeroboam was restored when the anonymous man of God entreated healing (1 Kings 13:1-10). The widow's dead child was raised to life when Elijah pleaded for mercy (1 Kings 17:17-24). At the request of Hezekiah, God delivered Israel from the wicked Assyrian king, Sennacherib (2 Kings 19). And Ezra's prayer for safety was granted when the Jewish exiles returned to Jerusalem (Ezra 8:21-23).

Prayers continued to be answered in the New Testament, as well. Through prayer, Zechariah and Elizabeth conceived a son (Lk. 1:13). Tabitha was raised from the dead (Acts 9:40). Countless petitions were made to the physical Person of Jesus Christ, God's Son, and the miracles that resulted were numberless. Lepers were healed (Lk. 17:11-19). Storms ceased (Lk. 8:22-24). Paralytics were made whole (Matt. 9:1-8). Blind received sight (Mk. 10:47-52). Demons departed (Mk. 9:14-29). Sick people were cured (Mk. 5:21-43). And the deaf could hear, and the mute could speak (Mk. 7:31-35).

"Now there are also many other things that Jesus did. Were every one of them
to be written, I suppose that the world itself could not contain the books that
would be written" (Jn. 21:25).

Following the life and death of Jesus Christ, the local church was established. Prayer was an integral and expected part of this new institution. The early church faced great persecution and was especially hated by the Jewish community. One ruler, Herod Agrippa (who was part Jew himself), sought hard to gain favor among his people. Upon the execution of James, the brother of John, his approval numbers increased. So, he also arrested Peter, the leader of the early church. He desired a pubic trial, followed by another execution. Peter was placed under high security and guarded by four soldiers at all times. Herod remembered that Peter had already been miraculously freed from prison once before, and he intended to prevent another such occurrence (Acts 5:17-18).

"So Peter was kept in prison, but earnest prayer for him was made to God by the church" (Acts 12:5).

As Peter slept soundly on the night before his trial, an angel appeared. He loosed Peter's chains, led him past the four guards on duty, and opened the iron gate at the entrance of the prison (Acts 12:6-17). God heard and mightily answered the direct prayers of the church for Peter's release.

I trust that it is becoming abundantly clear that God answers prayer. He acts for both the courageous and the fearful (Matt. 14:28-33), the young and the old (1 Sam. 17), the mighty ruler (Josh. 10), and the dying thief (Lk. 23:42-43).

He listens to doubts and demands just as carefully as He listens to shouts of courage and worship. He graciously welcomes each petitioner and bends His ear toward every voice. He is always accessible (Jer. 23:23-24), always attentive (Psa. 10:17), always faithful (Psa. 119:90), and always kind (Psa. 36:7).

Lastly, God *delights* in the prayers of His children (Prov. 15:8 NLT). Can you even comprehend that? He actually enjoys them! The Creator of the universe cares deeply for His creation and desires an intimate relationship with each one. He numbers every hair (Matt. 10:30), notices every tear (Psa. 56:8), and observes every thought (Psa. 139:2).

He is interested in every step, every sleep, and every word of every life. He watches every embryo grow and every bone develop (Psa. 139). And He wants to hear your every prayer (Phil. 4:6; 1 Thess. 5:17).

Make no mistake about it. **God loves you deeply**!

In Genesis, He spoke everything into existence, then watched as His creation betrayed Him. But rather than dooming us to the death we deserved, He sent His only Son, Jesus Christ, to Earth to reconcile man to Himself. Despite our violent rejection of this Redeemer, God accepted His perfect sacrifice on man's behalf. And today, He actively listens to the risen Savior, Who faithfully brings the prayers of the saints before His Kingly throne.

And sometimes when you pray, God gives you exactly what you ask for. Sometimes, He grants pennies to the preschooler. Sometimes, He gives romance to the rejected. Sometimes, He gives courage to the coward. Sometimes, He gives healing to the hopeless.

Such moments will take your breath away. They will put an unspeakable joy in your heart and a song on your lips. They will remind you of God's presence in your life and His infinite care for every detail of it. They will boost your confidence in the power of prayer and in the God Who turns His ear away from the angels' worship in Heaven to listen to the simple pleas of His beloved petitioner. Hold on to those moments. Write them down. Testify of them publicly. And never forget that God hears and answers your prayers.

CHAPTER TWO

SOMETIMES GOD GIVES PEACE IN THE PRESENT

"Do not be anxious about anything, but in everything by prayer and supplication with thanksgiving let your requests be made known to God. And the peace of God, which surpasses all understanding, will guard your hearts and your minds in Christ Jesus" (Phil. 4:6-7).

"WHAT DO YOU MEAN YOU can't see anything?" my mother pleaded frantically.

"It's completely black. I can't see it," I replied with much less enthusiasm.

Her panic increased, and she commanded, "Heidi, this is serious. Now, you cover your left eye and try again. What am I holding in my hand?"

But while I was fully aware that my mom was holding up our bright blue copy of *The Cat in the Hat* and waving it back and forth in rapid motion, I simply could not see anything at all with my right eye.

"Mom, I can't see it. It's all black," I repeated.

Early on in life, my severe nearsightedness was discovered—legal blindness, in fact. By age two, I already wore thick glasses; and before starting kindergarten, I received contacts. Every morning, my mom put them in; and every evening, she took them out and cleaned them. I had almost nothing to do with the process, except for the clear instructions that if a contact ever came out, I was to bring it straight to her.

And that was exactly what I did that warm, fall day in Minnesota. I had been playing in the wooded area behind our house with my sister and some neighborhood friends when a tree branch swiped across my eye and knocked my contact out. I calmly brought it inside to my mom, hoping that she could quickly remedy the situation so that I could return to building forts and obstacle courses with my friends. But that day, after cleaning off my contact, she briefly asked if she could take a moment to check my vision.

At only seven years old, I had been making comments from time to time that I wasn't seeing correctly. Black floaters and flashes of light entered my field of vision. However, despite these inconveniences, I was relatively unconcerned and went about my daily life as normal.

Anxious to just get this vision test over with, I reluctantly walked into the family TV room and plopped down into a comfortable, brown recliner. And that is where the sudden realization occurred that I had far greater problems than nearsightedness. That is where I discovered for the first time that my right eye had gone completely blind. And that is where I learned that this was a much bigger deal than my young mind initially thought.

The next few hours exploded into panic as my mother frantically took action. With my dad still twenty minutes away at work, my mom ran to the neighbor's house and requested an immediate ride to the hospital. She pestered me with questions throughout the drive and into the cold emergency waiting room. Upon finally seeing the doctor, we received the verdict that my retina was completely detached and was floating around loose inside my eye. Surgery was scheduled immediately, and strict instructions were given for my care.

This entire incident truly shook my mother to the core. Her mind raced with fear; her whole body was affected as she continually expected the worst. In her nearly paralyzed state, it was my dad who brought me to the hospital for my first major surgery. After dressing me in my hospital gown, he held me in the waiting room and fervently prayed for God's power. Eventually, the doctor arrived and escorted me and my teddy bear down the long hallway into the operating room. The surgery team was so gentle as they lifted me onto the table and tucked blankets all around my cold body. Then, the bubble-gum-flavored anesthesia was administered, and the three-hour surgery began.

During the operation, my retina was reattached; a silicone buckle was attached to the perimeter of my eye; and a gas bubble was placed inside the cavity for support. This was followed by several days spent recovering in the hospital and a couple weeks of laying totally face-down in bed to promote healing. The anesthesia took a major toll on my body, and I missed an entire month of school while coming off of it. But despite all the drama, healing finally occurred, and some of my vision was eventually restored.

Following this major ordeal, life slowly returned to normal. We proceeded with a bit more caution and made regular eye check-ups a priority. But then, just one year later, it happened all over again in my other eye. There was another total retinal detachment. There was a repeat surgery with another silicone buckle attached to my left eye. There were several days in the hospital and several weeks spent lying face-down in bed. There was another month off of school. There were countless cards and gifts delivered to me from those who cared. And thankfully, there was not as much permanent vision loss this time around, since the discovery was made much sooner, and the problem was addressed immediately.

Very few answers were given as to the cause of these eye problems. While several theories were offered, it seemed, in many ways, to be a mystery. And so, while much private research was done by my mother, and a few more carrots were added to my diet for overall eye health, we were really forced to leave this matter in the hands of God.

Two years passed by without any incident. I was now ten years old and loved my fifth-grade life down in Tempe, Arizona. My teacher, Mrs. Woods, became an all-time favorite of mine, bringing regular laughter and making learning fun. But that year, another milestone occurred—I received my first ever "C" on a report card. Being highly disappointed, my parents scolded and disciplined me. They questioned the sudden change in behavior. Knowing full well that eye problems usually brought instant compassion and pity, I expressed some difficulty reading the board at school. But this was quickly labeled an excuse when doctors assured them that everything inside my eyes was perfectly normal.

My grades continued to slip, and the frustrations continued to grow. While I may have used my eye problems at times to gain sympathy, the truth was that I really could not read much of anything that Mrs. Woods wrote down on the class whiteboard. Tests and quizzes were given on an overhead projector at the front of the room. But no amount of straining on my part brought the letters into focus. Time after time, questions remained unanswered, and empty papers were turned in. I assumed the doctors knew what they were talking about when their bright lights revealed nothing of concern. And so, my young mind concluded that the only problem that existed was me.

This continued on for several months until, finally, another retinal detachment was discovered. Emergency surgery was scheduled once again by the very doctor who had ignored my symptoms. To top that, during my recovery, we learned that the surgery was unsuccessful and would need to be repeated a second time. When the doctor who performed these surgeries died suddenly of "suspicious causes" shortly thereafter, we began to understand how personal problems in his life may have led to my misdiagnosis and faulty treatment. As a result of these setbacks, I permanently lost even more vision in my right eye.

Eventually, the drama subsided once again. Aside from a cataract surgery at age twelve, my eyes seemed to have settled down and stabilized. Doctors diagnosed several diseases and syndromes that they theorized I was born with and explained that the fluid in my eye was much thicker and stickier than normal. It somehow began to pull itself away from the back of my extremely elongated eyes (a process that normally happens in older age) and took the retina off with it. They hoped that once this vitreous fluid removed itself completely, further damage could be avoided.

And so, with hopeful hearts, we pressed forward in life. I received firm instructions to avoid activities in which I could potentially get hit in the head. Though an active child, I was not very athletic, and so, I wasn't bothered much by the fact that I most always had to sit on the sidelines at school recess and P.E. This simply became a new normal that I quickly embraced.

The next several years were probably some of the happiest of my entire childhood. I managed to stay out of the hospital for several years, and I thrived in the church youth group and Christian school that my sister and I attended. I was elected as class secretary for several years in a row and even made the varsity cheerleading squad as a freshman in high school. (What a perfect place for someone so used to standing on the sidelines during athletic events!) I had a number of extremely close girlfriends and, despite being only fifteen years old, I had a boyfriend that I was sure I was destined to marry. I earned straight A's in school and was quite popular among my peers. Yes, life was very good.

But at the end of my freshman year in high school, everything changed. God called our family to move away from this life I knew and loved. He directed us away from Tempe, Arizona, and all the way back north to frigid Owatonna, Minnesota, where my dad was offered a position at a small Bible college. While the internet and cell phones may have existed, our family certainly hadn't discovered these essentials just yet. This was truly and officially "goodbye" to the beautiful life and people that I loved.

The tears flowed and flowed. They flowed when I said my final farewells to all my close girlfriends. They flowed in uncontrollable sobs the night that I parted with my boyfriend, Adam. They flowed when only several months later, he called me "Erica" on the phone. (My name is NOT Erica!!!) They flowed as I faced the harsh reality that this long-distance, high school romance was over. They flowed as I realized that the wonderful life I had enjoyed in Arizona was moving forward without me. They flowed daily as I attended a new school that I hated. And they flowed when, only months after this major transition, my eye problems came back with a vengeance.

It was almost Christmas of 1996, and I was half-way finished with my sophomore year of high school. It was a cold Sunday morning in which we visited my uncle's church in the Minneapolis suburbs. But as I sat there in that bright red auditorium chair and listened to the message, my heart sank. I suddenly noticed a black veil beginning to creep across my field of vision once again. By now, I knew exactly what was happening, and my fears were confirmed when a trip to the emergency room revealed yet another retinal detachment.

By this point in my life, I had already experienced significant permanent vision loss in my right eye. But this detachment was in my left eye—my good eye. By the time I was called back into the exam room to see the retina specialist, half of my vision was completely gone, and darkness continued to grow with each passing hour. Because the retina had already come off the central portion of my eye around the optic nerve, the doctor expressed serious concerns about the ability to restore any vision at all. He patched both my eyes and gave firm instructions to lie perfectly still at home until emergency surgery could be performed first thing the next morning.

Following the appointment, my mom and I just sat in the parking lot and cried. The magnitude of this information was overwhelming. In an instant, I faced the reality that my future might be in total darkness.

After arriving home, I ate a small amount of dinner before going straight to bed. I tried to lie perfectly still and feared that any movement at all sealed my permanent fate of blindness. And I listened as my parents made numerous phone calls and asked Christians everywhere to pray for a miracle.

While I had already faced this dilemma a number of times in my younger life, this was the first time I had really experienced fear. My previous trials had included physical pain and discomfort but were also surrounded by the loving care and attention of my family and friends. I had been much younger and had very little concern about any long-term effects. But at this new stage in my life, such news played a much larger role.

That night, my future looked bleak, and my mind flooded with questions. How would I ever finish school without my eyesight? Could I go to college? Who would ever marry a blind girl? Would I be able to care for children someday, or would I be totally dependent on others?

The next morning, eye surgery number six proved to be successful. My retina was reattached, and over time, most of my vision was restored. But while we were grateful for this victory, such rejoicing ceased abruptly just two short months later when it happened all over again in my other eye.

Our family was enjoying a vacation on the East Coast when another black veil began to make its ominous appearance. Another emergency room. Another retinal detachment. Another operation. On March 1, 1997, I spent my sixteenth birthday in a hospital in Virginia recovering from eye surgery number seven. Nurses attempted to brighten my day with the worst lemon cake on the planet, which bore the inscription, "Congrats to the new mom." Missing our flights due to this medical emergency, my mom eventually drove us back to Minnesota in a rental car, while I laid face down in the back seat recovering.

While we faithfully hoped for the best, the worst seemed to follow. And follow. And follow. The next five months consisted of approximately ten additional surgeries. (Somewhere during this period of time, I actually lost track of the actual number.) The hospital became my home. Doctors filled my days. Pain was ever present. Medications replaced memories. And fear flooded my future.

At sixteen years old, I had hoped to obtain my driver's license that summer. But while I spent weeks at a time in a specialty chair designed to keep me face down, my younger sister completed the classes ahead of me. I longed for the life that once existed with the friends I held dear, but instead, I seemed to be surrounded by strangers in a place that wasn't home.

People around the country offered faithful prayers on my behalf. My sister, at age fifteen, even fasted as she pleaded for God's power. Hundreds of prayers were lifted. Prayer for strength. Prayers for relief. Prayers for healing.

One morning as I awaited yet another operation, I prayed aloud in the back seat of our car. My parents were still getting things ready inside the house, while I laid in total darkness alone. My mind swirled with questions as I feared my future. The tears flowed as I vocalized my pain and expressed my heartaches to God. I begged for mercy and a token of His power. I pleaded for healing and an end to all this struggle.

And in a moment that could never be forgotten as long as I live, God gave me peace. In an instant, my sorrow turned into security. During this period of greatest fear, God gave me the greatest calm. As I stared at a future filled with greatest darkness, my mind was turned toward greatest truth. God was in sovereign control of my life and was using these circumstances to accomplish His greatest good!

In those moments alone, the silence was replaced with singing as I confidently affirmed that God was molding a masterpiece within me (Rom. 9). What I experienced that day cannot be adequately expressed in words. It was truly a peace which surpassed all understanding (Phil. 4:7). It was *not* a peace that God would fix my physical problems and that my vision would be restored. It was not the assurance that I would be able to attend college, marry, and have children someday. It was not a confidence that things would be easy. It was a peace in my present. A peace that wholeheartedly believed that no matter what happened, I was going to be okay. The Potter was in Divine control, and He would answer my prayers as He deemed best.

* * *

What is peace? The Hebrew word *shalom* does not focus on the nega-tive—the removal of trouble. Instead, it positively declares peace as the high-est good in life. Biblical peace "enables believers to remain calm in the most wildly fearful circumstances. It enables them to hush a cry, still a riot, rejoice in pain and trial, and sing in the middle of suffering. This peace is never by circumstances, but instead affects and even overrules them."[1] A person filled with this kind of peace is not a victim, but rather aggressively attacks circum-stances in a supernatural and permanent manner.

"Peace I leave with you; my peace I give to you. Not as the world gives do I give to you. Let not your hearts be troubled, neither let them be afraid" (Jn. 14:27).

Do you know when Jesus Christ spoke these words? The very night be-fore He was to die in agony on the cross! He knew about His impending tor-ture and death. He knew how these events would change the entire course of the world. He knew that persecution awaited those who chose to follow Him. He knew what was coming, yet He spoke about peace!

Such peace is what allowed Paul and Silas to sing in the jail at Philippi (Acts 16:25). It is the reason that Paul stated that though he was dying, yet he had life. Though he endured sorrow, yet he rejoiced. And though he pos-sessed nothing, yet he possessed everything (2 Cor. 6:9-10). If all this positiv-ism wasn't enough, he went even a step further and chose to boast in his infirmities (2 Cor. 12:7). Literally, he found joy in them!

Now, let me remind you about Paul's life. He was imprisoned on numer-ous occasions for sharing the Gospel. While ministering to his own people, the Jews, Paul was punished by them with thirty-nine lashes on five differ-ent occasions. Three times, he was beaten with rods; and one time, he was stoned. While both actions were illegal for a Roman citizen, the law did little to protect Paul. "Three times, [he] was shipwrecked." And once, he was left "adrift at sea." Traveling constantly, he faced regular threats and dangers from robbers, false prophets, and his own countrymen. He endured regular "toil and hardship, through many a sleepless night, in hunger and thirst, often without food, in cold and exposure" (2 Cor. 11:27). He also faced the daily pressures and anxieties over his daunting workload for the churches. And this list, found in Second Corinthians 11:23-28, is not all-inclusive! It was written when Paul had completed only two-thirds of his earthly ministry! Certainly, these many sufferings continued until the end of his life. It is believed that Paul died by beheading at about age sixty-one in a Roman prison under the rule of Nero (A.D. 66).

Can you even begin to imagine the ongoing physical effects on Paul's body through his many years of persecution? And what about the mental effects from suffering so unfairly at the hands of his own Jewish community for his service to Christ? If anyone could claim victim status, it was Paul.

Certainly, Paul did not enjoy his suffering. In fact, we read in Second Corinthians 12:7 that he prayed and pleaded with God to remove some of it. And yet, when God replied that His grace was sufficient, Paul recommitted to an attitude of thankfulness and contentment.

"Do not be anxious about anything, but in everything by prayer and supplication with thanksgiving let your requests be made known to God. And the peace of God, which surpasses all understanding, will guard your hearts and your minds in Christ Jesus" (Phil. 4:6-7).

Guess who wrote that? Paul. The word "guard" is a military term meaning "to stand at a post; to guard against aggression."[2] And that is what the peace of God will do for those who bring their requests before God in prayer.

This was not something that came naturally. In Philippians 4:11, Paul said, "I have *learned* in whatever situation I am to be content" (emphasis mine). Several verses later, he affirmed that such peace could be found only through God's strength (Phil. 4:13). Through this supernatural power, he had learned to place little value on his earthly life and chose to focus on the eternal goals instead (Acts 20:24).

O LORD, my heart is not lifted up;

my eyes are not raised too high;

I do not occupy myself with things

too great and too marvelous for me.

But I have calmed and quieted my soul,

like a weaned child with its mother;

like a weaned child is my soul within me.

(Psa. 131:1-2)

For me, those moments in the back seat of the car were not the last time I would experience the glorious gift of peace. Many additional surgeries followed. Many more uncertainties about my future continued. The permanent loss of sight in my right eye eventually resulted. There were periods of time in which problems with my other eye rendered me legally blind and unable to fully function. There were many more fears, tears, and frustrations. But God has faithfully continued to give me peace!

During one particular time period of uncertainty, I penned the words to a song I titled, "Give Me Eyes That See." The chorus has remained the desperate prayer of my heart.

God, give me eyes that see Your matchless goodness in the plan You made for me,

Eyes that see the love that kept Your Son on Calvary's tree,

Eyes that see the Spirit's power to live triumphantly.

Open my vision, Lord, and give me eyes that see.[3]

In His goodness, God has used this physical trial in my life to teach me more about His Sovereign and eternal plan. He has taught me that sometimes healing is *not* the best thing for me. And time and time again, He has granted the supernatural gift of peace in response to my countless prayers.

Dear child, God can do this for you, too. He can give you peace and acceptance right in the middle of your trial. A mind at rest. A perfect calm. A beautiful trust in your Sovereign, Heavenly Father. There are people today who possess all the health, wealth, and prosperity one could ever imagine, yet they do not have peace. Imagine having this ultimate gift—this greatest good—right in the midst of the unimaginable. Talk to God. Tell Him your fears. Ask Him your petitions. And understand that God may choose to change *you*. He just might choose to answer your prayers by blessing you with the unspeakable treasure of peace in your present.

"But the meek shall inherit the land and delight themselves in abundant peace"

(Psa. 37:11).

CHAPTER THREE

SOMETIMES GOD WANTS ME TO WAIT

"It is good that one should wait quietly for the salvation of the LORD. It is good for a man that he bear the yoke in his youth. For the LORD will not cast off forever, but, though he cause grief, he will have compassion according to the abundance of his steadfast love; for he does not willingly afflict or grieve the children of men" (Lam. 3:26-27, 31-33).

THE CAMP CHAPEL VIBRATED WITH deafening screams as the director exultantly awarded points for each item collected in that evening's team scavenger hunt. Individuals from both corners sprinted to the front as he called out for their collection of pine cones, rocks, and bird's nests. One hundred points here. Five hundred points there.

"Next, we need the live worms," he hollered into his megaphone. Two teenage boys proudly bolted to the center stage, holding their brown, slithering creatures triumphantly for all to see. The girls squealed in disgust, while the boys roared with prowess. The noise level reached epic levels as the director shouted, "One thousand extra points to whoever eats their worm!"

The room watched in disbelief as a tall, skinny, brown-haired boy named Rob threw his live worm into his mouth and jerked his body from side to side as he tried to swallow it whole. His heroism that night gained victory for his team and a lasting impression on many.

I continued to see Rob from time to time at various church functions around Minnesota—family camp, athletic events, youth activities. His six-and-a-half-foot frame and his large personality often made him the center of attention. He seemed to always be singing a solo or leading a group game somewhere. He always had a girlfriend. And he always had duct tape. Truthfully, I possessed little interest at all in this boy. We had never had any sort of real conversation. I knew him, and he knew me. Nothing more. That is, until February of 1999.

Having struggled greatly with our major move to Minnesota and especially with my new school, my parents eventually enrolled me in a post-secondary program at Pillsbury Baptist Bible College, where they both worked. As a seventeen-year-old senior, I became a full-time freshman in college. I moved into the dorms and attended all the regular classes. And Rob's older sister just so happened to be my roommate.

I made friends quickly at college and loved this new environment. Despite my young age, I did well academically. After auditioning for an elite vocal ensemble, I traveled with this group on most weekends.

I also had a pretty big crush on a certain red-headed boy. He and I were among a small handful of music majors, and so we had most of our classes together. And one particular weekend in February, his handbell choir was scheduled to play at Rob's church in New Ulm, Minnesota. I selflessly offered to give my roommate a ride home that weekend.

While my motives may have been less than pure, I did have a good time as I became acquainted with their family. Sunday arrived, and the handbell concert was great—though I paid little attention to the music. And after the church service, I was ready to return to the dormitory.

But Rob's sister begged me to stay just a little bit longer. She wanted to eat pizza and to watch a movie with her family. And so, I reluctantly obliged. Sitting downstairs in their cold basement, we munched on snacks and watched the old classic *The Lion, the Witch, and the Wardrobe*. My mind was a million miles away as it focused on romantic dreams about the one I secretly came to see. But about halfway through the movie, I was jolted back to the present when the long, cold fingers of a different boy began to weave themselves into mine.

I was paralyzed in stunned disbelief to realize that Rob Fuller was holding my hand. Within moments, our fingers were gently connected—a position they remained in for the next thirty minutes. This was Rob Fuller, whom I had talked to for the first time that weekend. Rob Fuller, whom I had disregarded and even laughed at for the past several years. Rob Fuller—the center of his own universe—who ate worms and idolized duct tape.

And I reciprocated his boldness. My mind swirled as I sat there in total shock. I vacillated between excitement over this gesture and distaste for such arrogance. I remained silent as I watched the movie and wondered what in the world I would do when it ended. And then it did.

As the credits rolled, we stood up from our recliners and headed upstairs in total silence. We placed our dishes in the kitchen sink and then walked outside to say our goodbyes. I loaded my car and prepared to make the hour-long drive back to school. And in one of the most awkward moments of my life, Rob whispered in my ear, "Can I email you sometime?"

For good or bad, that was how it all started. Rob was sixteen years old and a junior in high school, and I was seventeen. Our regular correspondence via email eventually graduated to phone conversations. And before long, I drove to his house almost every Friday night to spend the entire weekend with his family.

We took frequent walks together throughout the various state parks and gardens of his beautiful hometown. We enjoyed regular movie and pizza nights. And we both actively served the Lord at First Baptist Church of New Ulm, Minnesota, where Rob's dad was the senior pastor. This unusual high school romance continued to grow and blossom for the next three-and-a-half years.

Now, anyone who knows either of us well at all knows that we both love to talk. (Ironic, since our relationship began without any communication.) In fact, we used to joke that during our dating years, we had pretty much discussed every possible topic in the universe. We talked about our spiritual values and biblical roles in the home. We discussed finances and future goals. We shared our career dreams and plans for achieving them. And we created a picture of what we desired our family portrait to look like someday. Yes, we certainly had a unified vision for our future and a path that we hoped would get us there.

And so, just two short weeks after I graduated college with my bachelor's degree in music education and Bible, Rob and I were married at the ripe ages of nineteen and twenty-one. On May 25, 2002, we glowed with delight at our double wedding with my sister, Heather, and her husband, John. What a spectacular day! Giving their only two children away at the same time, my parents spared no expense for this momentous celebration. We spent the day surrounded by 425 of our closest family and friends. Fragrant bouquets of peach and white flowers filled the large auditorium in Plymouth, Minnesota. Candles flickered in glass bulbs down the elaborately decorated center aisle. Sage green fabric created a delicate backdrop across the entire stage. The music was glorious and seemed to fill the entire sanctuary.

After the ceremony, the large crowd was invited to a full-course, sit-down dinner of delicious foods, while being serenaded by a live variety of classic love songs. Two large cakes shaped as grand pianos adorned the dessert table, located adjacent to the punch fountain. My mother had spent the entire year making flower arrangements, curtains, linen tablecloths, cloth napkins with matching rings, and gorgeous sage and peach centerpieces for each table. There was no doubt about it—this was the wedding of every girl's dreams!

Rob and I spent the following week honeymooning in beautiful Mackinaw Island, Michigan. This unique location in the upper peninsula proved to be the perfect place to relax after all the wedding festivities. We rented a tandem bike and rode around the island, which was noted for its absence of motored vehicles. We toured Fort Mackinaw and bought bright orange sweatshirts in the gift shop. We found a quaint little ice cream shop and enjoyed eating our humongous cones while watching the sun set over the Mackinaw Bridge. It was the perfect beginning to our new life together!

Upon returning home, we had so much fun opening all our wedding presents and setting up our cute, little two-bedroom apartment together. As young newlyweds, we quickly established a routine and became active as a couple in our local church. Besides my full-time job as the teller supervisor of a bank, I immersed myself in decorating our home and learning how to cook. Rob kept busy with his early morning job at UPS and his afternoon work as a computer tech at Pillsbury Baptist Bible College. With two years of undergraduate school still remaining, activities only increased for him in the fall with the start of classes and the new college basketball season. Despite his very busy schedule, he achieved his highest grade point averages after marriage and was even voted MVP of the college basketball team for three years in a row.

On the weekends, we loved biking and being spontaneous together. We had the freedom to watch movies until one o'clock a.m. or make late night runs to Dairy Queen. We tried our hand at home renovations, replacing our kitchen floors and even spray painting our appliances.

Then, just following our one-year wedding anniversary, we were hired by our Bible college to travel for ten weeks with two other young married couples across the United States as student reps. Our group, Voices of Victory, sang at concerts and promoted the school in five to seven churches each week. Aside from meeting fellow Christians all over the country, we enjoyed some amazing sightseeing on our days off. We hiked through the beautiful trails of Duluth, Minnesota. We went tent camping in the mountains of Colorado. We celebrated the Fourth of July at a spectacular fireworks show and live orchestra concert in Denver. We spent a day at Six Flags, Elitch Gardens; another day learning to golf on the greens in beautiful Idaho; and another day rappelling in the majestic mountains of Montana. We toured Mount Ranier National Park and went skim boarding and scooter racing along the beaches of the Pacific Ocean. We visited the iconic Public Market Center at Pikes Place in Seattle and a 747 airplane manufacturing plant in Everett, Washington. We attended a Mariners baseball game and tasted sushi, octopus, squid, and salmon roe at an elaborate seafood buffet called Todai's. (Okay, by "we," I mean most everyone else except me.) And the list could literally go on and on. This exciting summer was truly a once-in-a-lifetime opportunity, as we traveled and served the Lord together, while making many lasting friendships and memories.

And then, we returned home once again. The adventures were replaced with academics and the excitement with education. Rob was about to enter his final year of Bible college, where he was majoring in both Bible and Music. He dove directly into his senior voice recital and ministry resumé preparations.

Now, our original timeline for life had clearly specified that we wanted to wait to have children until we had been married for at least three years. We had desired to have some time to just be a couple, as well as some time to save money, purchase a home, and get established in a full-time ministry position. But all of a sudden, something changed. It may have been the fact that our summer of fun was now over and we were returning back to "normal" life. It may have been because one of the couples we traveled with actually got pregnant the last week of our music tour. Or maybe we just craved something else that was new and exciting. But our minds had indeed changed, and our desires for a baby came upon us with a vengeance. After all, we had an extra bedroom in our apartment and only eight months left until graduation. We had money in our savings account and jobs that supported us. We had good insurance coverage and families who lived close by. Why did we need to wait? All of our friends seemed to be having babies, so why should we wait? Whatever the reasoning was, somewhere around September of 2003, the baby bug hit—big time. And so, our original plans were altered, and we eagerly began working toward this new and exciting goal—parenthood.

There were certainly disappointments as months one, two, and three passed by without success, but there was still hope. Christmas came with an announcement from my younger sister that they would be blessing my parents with their first grandchild. The smiles and congratulations I expressed to her tried to mask the growing desires of my heart and the disappointment that I had not been the first one to achieve this milestone. After all, I was the older sister. Wasn't it also my place to have the first grandchild?

Heather and I had always been very close. We shared a bedroom our entire lives growing up at home and spent many late nights talking, singing, and laughing. We were cheerleaders together in high school. We worked together at our local Perkins Family Restaurant and Bakery. And we walked many miles home from school together in the freezing snow. We took driver's training classes together. We both failed our driver's test the same day. We both passed our driver's test the same day. This togetherness only continued throughout college, where we were roommates. Our dorm room proved to be the hub of much life and hilarity. We cleaned the dorm bathrooms together on weekends, and on one very memorable occasion, almost flooded the women's third floor. We traveled together on college music groups, both during the school year and on several summer tours, as well. And, as previously mentioned, we even got married together in a double wedding.

But now, things were different. I seemed to suddenly have little in common with my lifelong friend. I no longer related to her or understood what she was going through. Months four, five, and six passed by for us without success of achieving pregnancy. As I spoke with my sister one evening, she relayed the emotional journey she had experienced when two whole months had yielded negative pregnancy tests for her. But now, her belly continued to grow, while we faced the growing disappointment of months seven, eight, and nine. Our lives now seemed so many worlds apart.

My relationship with my mom also changed. She was one of the few people in my life who knew that we were actively trying to conceive. She knew that with each milestone in my sister's pregnancy, the pain only increased for me. Whether it was the gender reveal or the baby shower, she seemed to constantly be torn between expressing happiness for Heather or empathy for me. And while I appreciated her desire to be sensitive to my feelings, I hated being the object of pity. I hated making others feel uncomfortable. I hated being the source of problems.

As the months continued to roll by, it seemed that all of our church friends were also having babies. At one Sunday school activity, I was the only lady in the group who was not a mother. I was becoming increasingly aware of the fact that I was different. As the women all congregated together in the kitchen, the conversation quickly turned toward children. They talked about everything from pregnancy symptoms to childrearing. And as they all chattered happily away, I found myself unintentionally excluded. I possessed nothing to contribute. I had no experience. I was not part of this group. I did not fit in. As Rob and I walked to our car later that evening, I began to cry. I sobbed the entire way home and began to wonder if it would ever be my turn.

As the school year wound to a close, other excitements entered the scene—graduation, Rob's senior music recital, the candidacy process and acceptance of a youth and music pastor position at a church in Berne, Indiana, and the signing of papers on a brand-new home to be built there. All the packing to move and the graduation festivities were great distractions from the longings in our heart for a child.

In May, 2004, just weeks after Rob's graduation, we loaded up a moving truck and excitedly headed out on yet another adventure—a new life in Indiana. We were thrilled to watch all the daily activity of our new home being built. I once again enjoyed all the shopping to furnish and decorate this new place. New relationships were formed, and friendships were established in our new church ministry. Hopes were high that a new baby would soon enter our lives.

But before we knew it, two long years had passed by without any success. By the twenty-fourth month of trying, the disappointment seemed to be endless. We finally sought out medical help and were soon being tested for all possible forms of infertility. Our lives soon revolved around ovulation charts, basal body temperatures, and invasive tests and procedures. A sense of dignity was lost as doctors asked many personal questions about our sex life and studied our private body parts. There were numerous times that I laid exposed on an exam table before a team of doctors and nurses, all in the hopes that something could be found.

With each new procedure or prescribed medication came the great hope that things would now be different. With each new symptom came the certainty that something finally worked. My mind soon became consumed with each late period and began to analyze every little twinge of discomfort. There were many months in which I was absolutely certain that I was pregnant. And each time, I possessed a glow as I dreamed about how the announcement would be made to my family and friends. Yet time after time, month after month, the pregnancy tests revealed truth. Great hopes and excitement were soon followed by excruciating periods—both physically and emotionally.

Finances also became an issue. Money flowed from our savings account into numerous doctor appointments and fertility treatments. Funds dwindled quickly. It seemed that any sense of security we had was thrown at a far-away dream. After several thousand dollars had been poured into tests, medications, and procedures, a diagnosis of "unexplained infertility" was finally given.

Discouragement now took a firm hold. In many ways, a diagnosis of anything would have been better than this. Even the knowledge that we were totally infertile would have been accompanied by some sense of finality. But "unexplained infertility" still left the door open. Doctors never told us that we couldn't have children someday. They were simply unable to identify the problem. They suggested that different procedures may bring success, but each new suggestion came with a great cost. It seemed so unfair that what we wanted so desperately appeared to come so easily for everyone else.

"What am I doing wrong?" was the question at the forefront of my mind. If doctors couldn't find anything biologically wrong, then it must be me. Each month, Rob and I would try something new. A new time. A new position. A new frequency. Our sex life became nothing more than a job with a goal to attain. Any sense of passion and spontaneity had vanished. Any enjoyment had simply flown out the window, along with everything else—our passion, our time, our money, our sense of control.

The empty nursery in our beautiful new home glared at me daily. It served as a constant reminder that I didn't work. That I was broken. That something was missing. That our home was incomplete.

On one day in particular, I hopped into our silver Oldsmobile Cierra and took a long drive alone through the rural farmlands of Indiana. As I drove through the quiet Amish community that surrounded our town, I listened to a recording of one man's personal testimony through tragedy. The preacher told of a house fire that had devastated his family, leaving his wife and daughter with severe burns and handicaps. He spoke of all the things that were lost on that dark day in his life. Loss of freedom. Loss of limbs. Loss of physical beauty. His story went on to speak of how God had used these losses to create great beauty.

But as I sat there sobbing through his testimony, I wondered about my own life. I had not experienced anything even remotely close to what he had endured. What had I lost? Why was this battle with infertility so hard for me? Why was it so painful? I slowly began to realize the depth of my personal struggle.

You see, infertility *is* a loss. It is the long, slow, painful death of a dream. It is the loss of hope for the life you had always pictured for yourself. It is the gradual realization that you may never feel a son in your womb or hold the hand of a little girl who resembles your features. It is the loss of control over your life and its destiny. It is the loss of relationships as they once were. It is the loss of standing in your circles—a movement from included member to an object of pity.

Infertility does not easily allow for closure. Just when acceptance seems to be on the horizon, another pregnancy announcement is made, or another baby is born. You see all around that parenthood is the normal result of marriage. On top of all this, you receive monthly reminders of your brokenness. With each new stain of blood, you remember the loss. You remember the dreams. You relive the pain.

Infertility is generally a private struggle. Most women do not desire to advertise this weakness. It often brings humiliation. Shame accompanies the admission that such distinctly female properties do not work. Stigma comes with claiming the label "infertile."

Infertility can also bring much guilt. Insecurities arise that your spouse must secretly long for someone else to fulfill this marital duty. It creates imaginations that a biological heir might be possible apart from you. Fears follow that resentment toward you must exist. And doubts begin to make you wonder if your marriage is cursed.

During this difficult time in my life, the tears flowed regularly, and the questions abounded. We were now the only couple in our church without children, and there didn't seem to be any change in sight. But while the losses seemed to be unending, the prayers only increased.

"Lord, please let this be the month that I get pregnant," I simply prayed repeatedly. Day and night, I faithfully pleaded with God. The doctors gave no indication that I couldn't ever get pregnant, and so the answer to my prayers seemed to be "wait." "Not now." "This isn't the best time."

While all of this was going on in our marriage, our ministries at the church were also struggling. Rob was fresh out of college and only twenty-two years old. He served full-time as the youth and music pastor of our church. I worked alongside him any way I could. While the music ministry came naturally to us both, the youth ministry did not. We worked tirelessly to succeed but were often reminded of our inadequacies. Despite our very best efforts, we seemed to be met only with the harsh criticism of others. We worked hard to plan and prepare exciting activities. We took teens on college and mission trips across the country and had them in our home regularly. We visited their schools and became involved in their personal lives. But it never seemed to be enough. The accusations were harsh and persistent.

There were many late nights together that we laid in bed and cried out to God for direction. We begged Him to change our circumstances or lead us to another ministry. One week in particular, we fervently sought God's wisdom as to whether or not Rob should turn in his resignation. But at the end of that week, God clearly reminded us, "If you love those who love you, what benefit is that to you? For even sinners love those who love them. And if you do good to those who do good to you, what benefit is that to you? For even sinners do the same" (Lk. 6:32-33). While it would have been easier to leave, it seemed clear that God wanted us to wait in this area of our lives as well. To endure. To trust. To pray.

Isn't waiting sometimes the hardest part of prayer? Dwelling in the unknown? Living in the wilderness of uncertainty? While in waiting, it remains a mystery how God will one day answer your request. Waiting highlights your helplessness. It delays your dreams. It crushes your control. It steals your security.

And that is a good thing!

Nowhere in Scripture does God promise to give us exactly what we request each time we pray. God does not promise to grant our every heart's desire. And He certainly does not operate on our timetable. Rather, God promises to give us what is good (Rom. 8:28). And, believe it or not, sometimes waiting is a very good thing.

"It is good that one should wait quietly for the salvation of the LORD. It is good
for a man that he bear the yoke in his youth" (Lam. 3:26-27).

I used to view this time of waiting in my life as one of incompleteness and stagnation. It seemed that we were just existing, but never advancing, only waiting for what was to come.

But looking back on this time period, the benefits become obvious. Our marriage and ministries were greatly strengthened through this time of waiting. We learned how to share each other's burdens. We learned how to grieve together. We learned how to pray together. We gained compassion and sensitivity for others. We learned endurance. We learned how to better love our enemies. We learned that our plans are not always God's plans. We learned trust. We learned dependence. We learned surrender. We learned that God alone knows what is best for our lives.

* * *

Many individuals throughout Scripture also endured great periods of waiting. And much good resulted. In the midst of their own infertility, Abraham and Sarah were promised heirs as innumerable as the stars of the sky (Gen. 22:17). Yet, they endured twenty-five years of silence before this promise was fulfilled. It wasn't until Abraham had reached the ripe old age of one hundred that Isaac was finally born. During this extended period of waiting, sin abounded as Abraham sought to speed up God's plan. An adulterous relationship. An illegitimate son. A young servant woman rejected and abandoned.

You might wonder how any of this resulted in good. But fast forward in Abraham's life to his ultimate test—when God asked him to offer this long-awaited son, Isaac, as a burnt sacrifice. At that moment in time, Abraham's unprecedented faith was revealed. After being assured of the reliability of God's promise, Abraham now possessed a deep confidence that even if his son died, he would be raised again from the dead (Heb. 11:17-19). God purposely waited until the birth of a child seemed physically impossible before He acted. Why? God wanted to leave no doubt of His miraculous role in the conception of this child, and He desired *to develop unwavering faith* in the life of Abraham.

Joseph saw visions as a young boy that one day his older brothers would bow down to him (Gen. 37:9). After revealing this dream to them, they spitefully sold him into slavery and lied about the whole incident to their father. In Egypt, Joseph was unfairly accused of an assault on Potiphar's wife and endured several years in prison as a result. But because of his faithfulness and obedience to God even during those dark times, he was eventually released and promoted to the second highest ruler in Egypt. When a fierce famine devastated the land, Joseph's brothers traveled to Egypt in search of food. And there, twenty-two years after Joseph received the dream, they bowed down before him and begged for mercy.

Hatred. Jealousy. Attempted murder. A grieving father. Accusations. An unjust prison sentence. What good resulted from this period of waiting? It was all about *God's perfect timing.* Only God knew the exact moment that a deadly famine would arrive on the worldwide scene. He knew just when Joseph's family would journey to Egypt in desperation to find food. God arranged the events of Joseph's life so that at the perfect moment in time, he would be exactly where he needed to be to save the lives of his family and many others. All those sorrows and years of waiting, " . . . God meant it for good, to bring it about that many people should be kept alive . . . " (Gen. 50:20).

As a young boy, David was anointed by the prophet Samuel to be the next king of Israel (1 Sam. 16:13). But this anointing was followed by approximately fifteen years of waiting before he officially began to rule. During this time period, David returned to his work as a lowly shepherd boy. While in the fields, he improved in his writing and speaking abilities. He became skilled at playing the harp. He increased in strength and presence. He became valiant in war and fighting (1 Sam. 16:18). He was eventually called into the service of King Saul, where he ministered as both a court musician and eventually an armor-bearer. While there, he developed leadership abilities, formed alliances, and established his legitimacy. Only God knew the future of this young king. He alone knew what character traits David would need to be successful in leading Israel. And in His infinite wisdom, God knew how beneficial this period of waiting would be *to prepare him for the future.*

Let us also consider the New Testament account of Mary, Martha, and Lazarus (Jn. 11). Lazarus became sick and was near death. Knowing of the great love that Jesus had for their family, the sisters sent word to Jesus and begged Him to come quickly and provide healing. But what did Jesus do? He waited. In fact, He intentionally remained where He was for two more days before coming to be with them. It wasn't until Lazarus had been buried and in the tomb for four days that Jesus finally arrived on the scene with His disciples. He compassionately stood beside Mary and Martha at their brother's tomb. And in that moment, a beautiful glimpse of Jesus' humanity is revealed when we read, "Jesus wept" (Jn. 11:35). Then, in a tremendous display of His omnipotence, Jesus raised Lazarus from the dead.

Now Jesus easily could have come and healed Lazarus at the sisters' initial request, and the end result would have been the same—a healthy brother. But instead, Jesus knew that waiting was better. Why? So that the faith of those present would be quickened (Jn. 11:15). On that day, onlookers received something so much grander than the simple healing they had witnessed before. That day, they witnessed the impossible through a *magnificent display of God's power!*

Lastly, it is recorded that even Jesus Christ Himself waited for answered prayer. An innocent man, He was condemned to die by the very ones He came to save. Yet, shortly after the nails were driven into His hands, binding Him to the cross on Mount Calvary, He cried out, "Father, forgive them, for they know not what they do" (Lk. 23:34). He literally requested that His enemies would be pardoned and that God the Father would withhold their due punishment of eternal death. Jesus clearly knew that such salvation could come only as their minds were opened to the truth of who He really was and as they humbly acknowledged Him as their personal Lord and Savior. But while Jesus requested salvation, a sacrifice was required.

The crowds continued to mock, and the soldiers proceeded to jeer. And after several hours of unspeakable agony, Jesus finally died. His disfigured body was removed from the cross and buried in a tomb. If the story ended here, how hopeless life would be. But three days after His death, Jesus miraculously raised Himself from the dead! This miracle proved to be the most significant event in all of human history. As a result, the Good News of salvation spread rapidly. The pardon from sin was offered. The message of forgiveness was proclaimed.

Fifty days later, God established His church. Following another supernatural display of power, three thousand souls were forgiven on the day known as Pentecost (Acts 2:41). Some of the very persecutors who were present at Jesus' crucifixion were likely among the crowd that day. Their eyes were now opened. Their lives were forever changed. Their destiny was secured.

Even today, Jesus desires "that all should reach repentance" (2 Pet. 3:9). He longs to save all mankind and pardon all sins. He yearns for all eyes to be opened "to the knowledge of the truth" (1 Tim. 2:4). And He waits. Jesus patiently waits for each soul to humbly bow the knee before Him and accept His free gift of salvation.

There are so many lessons we can learn from Christ's example of waiting! We see through his life the perfect model of forgiveness. It is one thing to offer forgiveness to someone personally, but Christ asked *God the Father* to also forgive His betrayers. It is one thing to forgive a friend, but Christ even forgave His enemies. It is one thing to forgive *after* a trial is over, but Christ extended forgiveness right during the very moments of His greatest pain. It is one thing to forgive someone who has asked for it, but Christ offered forgiveness to those who saw no need. And He continues to offer such forgiveness still today.

I trust that you are beginning to see how very good waiting can be. These are just a few of its many potential benefits:

- To develop unwavering faith (Abraham)
- To achieve God's perfect timing (Joseph)
- To prepare for the future (David)
- To allow God's power to be displayed more magnificently (Lazarus)
- To teach us valuable lessons (Jesus Christ)

Waiting is *not* merely a holding pattern in your life! There is a purpose. And that purpose is always good.

> *"But they who wait for the Lord* **shall** *renew their strength; they* **shall** *mount up with wings like eagles; they* **shall** *run and not be weary; they* **shall** *walk and not faint"* (Isa. 40:31—emphasis mine).

Knowing that there is a purpose for your season of waiting does not necessarily make things easier. This verse clearly describes waiting as a time of weakness and weariness. But those who endure, waiting on the Lord, receive renewal and strength.

So, what about that long journey before the finish line? That point *before* the wings like eagles? When your mind is anxious and you question God's care? When your strength is gone and your heart is faint?

If I could go back in time to that difficult place in life and counsel myself, here is what I would say:

1) "Weeping may tarry for the night, but joy comes with the morning" (Psa. 30:5). As impossible as it may seem, your sorrow is temporary. It is only for a season. Sometimes, the waiting lasts a very long time. Healing does not always come to the afflicted. Reconciliation does not always come to the wayward. Marriage does not always come to the lonely. Children do not always fill the empty arms. But the *weeping* is temporary. Joy will come! You can see only the short "now" of your life. Trust in the God Who sees eternity, and cling to His promises. Watch Him turn the very thing that causes your deepest sorrow into the thing that brings you the greatest joy!

2) "See to it . . . that no 'root of bitterness' springs up . . . " (Heb. 12:15). This takes conscious work! When God is freely giving to everyone else what you desperately desire, it is easy to become bitter. But bitterness destroys. It turns your sadness into an ugly anger that pushes comforters away. It robs you of your joy and reduces your effectiveness. It makes you say things you will regret and breaks relationships that may never heal. Hurting friend, please do not make your situation worse by allowing bitterness to take root.

3) "Give thanks in all circumstances; for this is the will of God in Christ Jesus for you" (1 Thess. 5:18). There is always something to be thankful for! Satan craftily works to deceive you into believing that you possess greater trials than anyone else. I once thought that nothing could be worse in life than to remain childless. But as I look back, I actually envy certain aspects now. Freedom. Flexibility. Extra finances. More quality time with my husband. Satan has a cunning way of making you believe the lie that the current state of your life is incomplete. That others have it better than you. That you are a victim. But please know that you will never be content in a different place in life if you are not content in your present. Give thanks to God for His bountiful goodness. It is there. Take the time to focus on it.

I write these things with the utmost compassion. In many ways, I am the poster child for failure during my seasons of waiting. I like to plan out my life and be in control of my circumstances. Inherently, I believe that my plans are good. I am slow to see the profit in detours. It is only in looking back that I can notice the benefits.

"Therefore the Lord waits to be gracious to you, and therefore he exalts himself to show mercy to you. For the Lord is a God of justice; blessed are all those who wait for him" (Isa. 30:18).

This is one of my all-time favorite verses! It gives insight into the very nature of our holy God—a God Who is just waiting to show grace and mercy. He is active and present in each life. He *will* act! He proves this time and time again. When seasons of waiting seem unbearably long, hold fast to the promise that God is working in your life for *good*. He might be developing your faith, waiting for the perfect timing, preparing you for the future, waiting to display His miraculous power, or teaching you valuable lessons about Himself. He alone provides strength for the difficult journey and the hope to soar like eagles. Allow Him to rule. Remember His loving heart. Trust in His perfect plan. Sometimes, God wants you to wait.

CHAPTER FOUR

SOMETIMES GOD SEEKS MY SUBMISSION

"For my thoughts are not your thoughts, neither are your ways my ways, declares the LORD. For as the heavens are higher than the earth, so are my ways higher than your ways and my thoughts than your thoughts" (Isa. 55:8-9).

WHILE OUR PRAYERS FOR CHILDREN remained faithful, our arms remained empty. Our third wedding anniversary came and went; but our yellow, orange, and blue-striped nursery just sat there empty—an ever-present reminder of our unfulfilled desires.

Rob would often comment that we should begin to consider adoption. He had long dreamed of adopting a baby. In fact, even from the time he was in junior high school, he carried this desire. But honestly, Rob had a myriad of dreams. He wanted to get his pilot's license someday. He wanted to build a recording studio in our house. He wanted to travel to Egypt and see the great pyramids. So, this seemed to be just another dream on his very long, yet very unrealistic, list.

In some ways, it irritated me how quickly Rob was able to give up on our hopes of a biological child. In time, our infertility seemed to be something that did not even bother him at all. While he cared that his wife was hurting, he also seemed to possess a confidence that children would come to us in some form at some time, and he did not personally care how it happened. His mind was very open and excited about adoption.

But for me, it was a totally different story. Adoption was not part of *my* plan. It was not the image that I had for my family. It removed the very stamp of womanhood from my life—pregnancy. It stole the opportunity of eagerly watching my belly grow and feeling my baby's movement inside. It took away the milestones of gender reveal parties, maternity pictures, and the whole birthing experience. It erased the possibility of children who resembled our features. It required extra effort. Extra money. Extra time.

Adoption carried with it so many unknowns. Was the special bond between a mother and child something that could be possessed only by those who shared DNA? Would an adopted baby instinctively know that I was not their biological mom? What if they grew up to push me aside and seek out their "real" family? What if they resented the fact that they did not look like their parents? What if they came with problems?

In my little circle of worldly acquaintances, I knew only a handful of people who had adopted children. And truthfully, they were not positive images. The adoptive parents that I knew were different, and their children all seemed to have serious emotional baggage. In my highly arrogant mind, I did not desire to lower myself to be a member of this crowd.

I also feared the attitudes of others. I worried about the reaction of our parents and wondered if they could grow to love an adopted child as much as their other grandchildren. I worried that an adopted child would be viewed as second best and grow to be pitied. I worried that adoption would put a public spotlight on our inabilities to conceive. Everyone would know that we were . . . broken.

One evening, I received a phone call out of the blue from a long-time childhood friend. She and her husband had now been married for about four years and were also struggling with infertility issues. They were a godly couple, who were serving God in full-time church ministry and were actively seeking His will. I remember asking her if they had ever considered adoption. But her reply was not what I had expected. She explained how she felt that if

God closed the door for pregnancy, it was because He did not want them to have children at all. She said that adoption felt like kicking a door open that God had purposely closed, instead of simply accepting His plan for their life. As I hung up the phone later that night, I had even more questions. What if God didn't want us to have children at all?

Our lives continued to exist in this state of great uncertainty until one very memorable Sunday morning during the summer of 2005. Our pastor was on vacation that week, and another godly man was filling the pulpit. He delivered a message that I would never forget. It was not super deep or even anything that I had not heard many times before. But it was exactly what I needed to hear on that day. He spoke about submission.

Our lives certainly must have looked like the picture of submission. After all, we had left our family and familiarity to come and serve the Lord in full-time church ministry here in rural Indiana. We were actively involved in many different facets of the ministry—music, youth group, children's ministries. We were faithful in our personal Bible reading and prayer. All the outward signs pointed to a life devoted to Christ.

But that morning, as he spoke, I was struck between the eyes with just how sinful I really was. I specifically recognized it in two primary areas of my life. First, I saw my sin in regards to our church ministry. God had called us to this particular place, yet here I was, complaining that it wasn't good enough. He directed us to lead the music for these dear people, yet I felt our talents were being underutilized. He led us to this small-town youth group and sovereignly brought certain teens out to youth activities, but I was dissatisfied with the numbers. The truth was, I thought that God should be using our talents and abilities in a much bigger and more spectacular way.

The second area in which God was revealing my sin was in regards to growing our family. It was no accident that we were facing infertility. God had sovereignly ordained it for a good purpose. But rather than quietly resting in His ways, I was obsessed with my own desire for pregnancy. I was unwilling to open my mind to the fact that God might have other plans. I did not want to even consider that His perfect will for us might be to remain childless or to pursue adoption. At the root of the issue, I did not fully believe that His ways could truly satisfy and bring me joy.

As the organ music began to play during the invitation at the close of the service, I walked forward and knelt in the front pew of our auditorium. In those few quiet moments, with tears streaming down my face, I confessed to God my sins of stubbornness, pride, and selfishness. I handed Him my earthly dreams and desires. I asked Him to take control of my life and guide me in His ways. I recognized anew His direction in leading us to this church. I committed to Him that if He sent only one teen to each youth activity from that point forward, then I would give that one individual my very best. And most significantly, that day, I told God that I would give Him full reign over our family. I prayed that I would learn to accept His plan if it did not ever include children. But I also committed that I would open the door of my heart to adoption, if that was what He deemed best.

What a relief to finally let go of my desperate striving! To give up control. To consciously choose to let God direct my steps. To rest in the knowledge that He had a good plan for my life—a plan that was filled with true satisfaction and joy.

As Rob and I sat down for dinner that afternoon, I told him of my new commitments. He was thrilled to hear how God had worked in my heart and was eager for the next step in our journey. Almost immediately, we began to make phone calls and to seek information regarding adoption. While we did not know His perfect will, we desired to open up every avenue to His choosing.

Everything was so totally new to us. We knew almost nothing about adoption. We called one of the few places we knew anything about—Baptist Children's Home in Valparaiso, Indiana. This Christian organization was several hours away from our home and dealt primarily with helping troubled youth. However, they also had the opportunity each year to place a handful of babies into homes through adoption. Not knowing how the process normally worked, this seemed like a good place to start.

After making the initial phone call, we scheduled a face-to-face meeting with a representative just a few short weeks later. Each party drove halfway, where we met in the middle at a Wendy's fast food restaurant. There, the agent told us about the ministry of B.C.H. and explained the adoption process in more detail. The first step was to complete a home study to make us legally eligible for an adoption placement. This process would include a series of three in-home meetings to both approve our house as a safe dwelling place for a child and to offer further education and training for Rob and myself. We needed the fire department to come and check our home for fire safety. We needed to complete a variety of government background checks and have our fingerprints run through the local police department. We needed to get physical exams from our doctors to prove that we were capable of caring for a child. We needed to collect several years of completed tax returns and bank statements and provide proof of our ability to financially support a child.

Plus, there was a stack of paperwork that we were asked to fill out stating our personal preferences regarding the ethnicity, health, and background of a child. What disabilities were we prepared to deal with? Would we consider a baby who had limited prenatal care? What if the birth mom had used drugs or alcohol during her pregnancy? Did we want a newborn, or would we consider older children?

Lastly, we were asked to create three detailed photo albums to be shown to potential birth parents who were considering placing their children for adoption. It was to clearly portray life in our home and demonstrate our lifestyle, interests, and occupations. It also needed to include a personal letter from each of us written directly to potential birth parents.

It was further explained to us that there would likely be a period of much waiting. In fact, the average wait time for an adoptive family going through

B.C.H. was about two years. We were also told that if we got pregnant during this time of waiting, then our names would be removed from the adoption list, and other families would take priority.

While we left that initial meeting loaded down with a long checklist of jobs to complete, we were also filled with much anticipation. We began immediately working through our assignments and got our first in-home visit scheduled for mid-November. When that day finally arrived, we proudly handed over those tasks we had already completed, including the three photo scrapbooks that I had spent many hours preparing. The meeting went well and, due to the holiday season, our second in-home visit was scheduled for January.

It felt good to be actively working toward adoption, and our hearts became increasingly eager to see how God would direct. But due to all the uncertainties and the long periods of waiting, we kept our activities primarily a secret. In fact, the only people who even knew that we were pursuing adoption were our parents. We figured that we would need to tell others only if, and when, a baby came along. And in truth, a part of me hoped that since I had now submitted my dreams to God, He would give me what I truly wanted—a pregnancy.

For Thanksgiving, 2005, we found ourselves hosting both sides of our family from all over the country at our home in Berne, Indiana. Our parents, siblings, and their families all stayed with us for several days, which we filled with much activity. Festivities included the traditional holiday feast, bowling, a tour of Amish country, family game night, a music concert at our church, and much food and laughter.

One evening, we all sat in a large circle around our family room and shared testimonies of personal thanksgiving for what God had done in each of our lives the past year. I remember expressing a deep gratitude for my husband. My love for him had truly grown as I had seen him so lovingly and patiently come alongside me in my times of heartache and confusion. In those moments there together, I felt that our hearts were now unified and submissive to God's direction. Despite several years of unsuccessful striving, we now had a peace that we were exactly where He wanted us to be. And I was filled with thankfulness.

We had barely finished cleaning up from all our houseguests over the holiday when we received an unexpected phone call one day from our adoption agent at B.C.H. "You're never going to believe this," he said. "But I have a birth mom who has chosen you to adopt her unborn baby, and she wants to meet you guys in person."

My mind swirled with about a million questions all at once. We had just had our first meeting only two weeks ago! We were told that we would likely be waiting for two years! Our adoption home study wasn't even completed! We didn't have any baby furniture or clothes! How was this even possible when we thought it would be February before we were even *eligible* to be considered by birth parents? When was the baby due? Was it a boy or a girl? What in the world do you even say to a woman who is contemplating giving you her child? I had only just recently opened up my mind to the possibility of adoption. But now, here I was on the phone, scheduling a meeting with some woman named Abigail and some lawyer in Ohio named Megan, wondering what in the world was happening. Our B.C.H. agent offered to attend the meeting with us and to help guide our conversation. And so, in what seemed like a whirlwind of activity, we found ourselves only days later driving to Bowling Green, Ohio, for the interview of a lifetime.

We walked nervously into the small, dark lawyer's office that cold December day. We kindly shook hands with this very pregnant, twenty-eight-year old, complete stranger and her young lawyer. The air was quiet and tense. Abigail sat across the table from us in almost complete silence as we told her about ourselves and what life would look like for her child if placed in our home. We talked about our families, our church, and other support systems. We shared our desire for children and the long road of disappointment so far.

After almost an hour, we asked if she had any questions for us. Expecting to be bombarded with inquiries, we were surprised when, after a moment's pause to think it over, the only thing she asked was what our church believed in. Rob briefly explained that he was a pastor at a Bible-believing church in Indiana that held to the supremacy of Scripture. And that was it. She gave little indication as to her inner feelings toward us. She had no other questions.

And with that, the meeting was over. No identifying information had been given. No last names or locations. No phone numbers. The conversation had been very general and factual. Void of emotion. Toward the end of our visit, she told us that she was expecting a baby boy and believed he would be born very soon. We left with a great feeling of uncertainty, as Abigail had seemed so distant. In fact, as we left the office, I whispered to Rob, "We'll never hear from her again."

In truth, we would have been okay not hearing anything more from this stranger about her baby boy. Things had happened so quickly for us. Our minds had not even processed everything that was happening. And our hearts had not been given liberty to hope yet. We didn't even know what was supposed to happen next, but figured that God would work to accomplish what He deemed best.

The busyness of the holiday season again helped to keep our minds occupied. With parties, youth activities, and vacation prep, there was not a dull moment to spare. The week of Christmas, we loaded up our car and drove to visit our family in Minnesota. After several days were spent reconnecting with my side of the family, we transitioned to be with Rob's family on Christmas Day. And while there were a number of surprises for us under brightly colored ribbons, the biggest one of all came on December twenty-sixth!

After several weeks of silence since our meeting, we received a phone call the day after Christmas from Abigail's lawyer. She indicated that Abigail had some more questions for us and wondered if we could do a conference call together. With hearts pounding, Rob and I quickly gathered ourselves in the church office of First Baptist Church in New Ulm, Minnesota. When the phone finally rang, and all parties were connected together, we nervously said our hellos. Once again, we expected a long list of questions. This seemed only natural from one who was making such a monumental life decision. But after several moments of small talk, Abigail had only one thing she wanted to ask.

"You know how when you apply for a job, the employer has to choose you for the position," she began. "Well, in a way, you have to also choose the employer. You have to say that you want the job, too. Well, I just want to know—if I choose you to adopt my baby, would you also choose me?"

We were stunned. Was that all she wanted to know? Had she been rejected so much in her lifetime, that she didn't think we would even want her baby?

We very quickly assured her that nothing would make us happier than to adopt her child. We reminded her again of our commitment to this process and the joy we hoped it would bring.

She hesitantly began talking again. She explained her shortcomings and negative family history. She spoke of depression, alcohol abuse, and lack of education. She confessed that poor choices in her life brought her to this place. She wanted to make very clear that this is what *she* was bringing to the table. And she wanted assurance that we really wanted *this* child.

We again expressed our total devotion to this baby and confidently told her that no tainted background would affect our decision. After a few brief moments of silence, she replied, "Then I want you to be his parents."

The joyful tears flowed as those words rang in our ears. What a gift! What a surprise! What a miracle! God had worked so quickly and clearly in our lives to show us His perfect will. His ways were proving to be so very good.

While our hearts soared with elation, they were also filled with much shock. We were going to be parents! And with Abigail's assurance that this baby was coming in January, it was going to be very soon! It was time to start getting ready.

After hanging up the phone, we couldn't wait to share our exciting news with the world. We drove to the store and bought some balloons that proudly announced, "It's a BOY!" Then, we drove to the local grocery store, where Rob's mom worked as a clerk, and surprised her with the news that her very first grandchild was soon to arrive. Next, the phone calls went out to our siblings, our church, and other close friends.

Upon returning home to Indiana, we worked full throttle to get things in order. With January already upon us, and not one baby item on hand, we needed to get shopping. We purchased and set up the entire nursery in record-breaking time—one day. The nursery proudly displayed a brightly colored train theme, complete with a crib, comfy bedding and blankets, changing table, dresser, rocking chair, an alphabet train that hung on the wall, and a featured picture frame that highlighted the words of Proverbs 22:6: "*Train* up a child in the way he should go; even when he is old he will not depart from it" (emphasis mine).

Abigail had invited us to come along and participate in one of her final OB appointments. So, we both drove to Ohio again for this special meeting. We listened to the baby's heartbeat and talked with the doctor. Abigail proudly introduced us as her baby's parents and even gave us his ultrasound pictures. She also presented her birth plan for the day of delivery, which included her deep desire that we both be present in the delivery room and have permission to be involved in his care immediately after birth. She made her wishes clear to the doctors and hospital staff. She went out of her way to make this experience wonderful for us and to ensure that we were with him from the very beginning.

Then suddenly, January turned into February. An induction was scheduled at the hospital if the baby did not arrive soon. But finally, after several weeks of anxious anticipation, we received the awaited phone call at one o'clock a.m. on February 13, 2006. "Abigail is in active labor. You need to come to the hospital right away."

We quickly grabbed our prepared bags and began the two-hour drive in the dark of night. We were alert with much excitement, despite the complete lack of sleep. As we walked into the hospital lobby, I paused for a moment to touch up my hair and makeup in the restroom. I needed to look presentable. After all, I was about to meet my son!

We stepped off the elevator and onto the labor and delivery floor just after 3:30 a.m. While much of the space was silent, the nurses had clearly been waiting for our arrival and hurried us down the hall. We could hear Abigail crying out in pain as we stood just outside her door. The nurses quickly put up a small curtain and created a space for us near Abigail's head. A wave of relief seemed to wash over her as we entered the room, for within about five minutes of our arrival, the cries of a healthy baby boy filled the space. It almost seemed as though she had been intentionally waiting for us before making those final pushes toward deliverance.

Griffen Anthony Fuller was born at 3:54 a.m., weighing in at seven pounds, fourteen ounces. As per the birth plan, Rob was able to cut his umbilical cord and, after being cleaned and examined, he was placed in my arms. As I fed him his first bottle, I was overcome with God's goodness to me. What a gift! Just a few short months earlier, we had wondered if we would ever have children at all. And now here we were, holding the most perfect baby boy in the whole universe.

Abigail would need to spend two full days in the hospital recovering. And, according to Ohio law, there was a period of time she needed to wait before she could officially sign any legal paperwork. So, it was required that Griffen also remain in the hospital during this period. Abigail insisted that I be given a hospital bracelet, giving me access to his care in the baby nursery. I gave him his first bath and spent time rocking him and just staring into his sweet face. A cot was wheeled into Abigail's room, where I slept next to Griffen's crib and got up for his nighttime feedings. But also during those forty-eight hours, we were able to spend some time getting to know Abigail and her mom,

Norma, who had also come for moral support. We learned much about her background and growing-up experience. She shared some of her personal struggles and failures and how she had come to know that adoption was the right choice for her baby.

I will forever treasure that short time there together in the hospital. You see, after we left, we never heard from Abigail again. God had placed her in our lives for a brief moment in history to simply be the agent of one of His greatest gifts to us! Just months earlier, we didn't know anything at all about adoption. We didn't know what to pray for or what to ask. And yet, God, in His grace, presented us with one of the most perfect adoption scenarios possible. As we all hugged goodbye that Wednesday morning, there were no tears from anyone—just mutual love and gratitude for God's plan and guidance in this little boy's life.

We spent the next twenty-eight days living at the Holiday Inn Express in Celina, Ohio, awaiting the signed interstate adoption paperwork. It was twenty-eight days of no cooking, no cleaning, no entertaining. There was no postpartum, no physical recovery time, no hormonal swings. Just uninterrupted time of bonding with our newborn son and relaxing between feedings. There was a pool and a hot tub, plus a continental breakfast served every morning. And even including all these unexpected hotel costs, Griffen's entire adoption cost only about $7600—approximately one-third the cost of a normal adoption! God had indeed been abundantly good to us!

Upon finally returning home, we were showered by our church with love and support at a train-themed baby shower! The teen girls in the youth group hosted a Saturday morning brunch in which Griffen received over eighty presents! (Mommy had a part-time job writing all those thank you notes.)

Griffen soon became the featured sweetheart of the church and youth group. He was frequently passed around among the teens, and the older couples in the congregation gladly volunteered for church nursery duty. Being one of very few young children, he received plenty of attention, and each milestone was celebrated by all. One Wednesday night after church, a small crowd gathered in the church foyer and cheered as Griffen demonstrated his newest milestone—standing up on his own.

Then, on October 3, 2006, we made the two-hour drive to Valparaiso to finalize Griffen's adoption. As we stood before Judge Bradford in our coordinating red and blue fall outfits, he declared that this little bundle of joy was now legally ours. After taking our pictures and expressing our thanks to all involved in the adoption process, we left the courthouse with joy in our hearts and legal documents in our hands. As our little family drove home that day, I began to read aloud to Rob the official adoption decree. There was much legal jargon and other factual information involved in our case. But toward the very end were these words:

> "The minor child shall take the name of Griffen Anthony Fuller, and shall for all intents and purposes be considered the child of Robert & Heidi Fuller, and shall be entitled to the same rights and privileges which he would have been entitled to if he had been the natural child of Robert & Heidi Fuller."

By this point, the tears were flowing down both of our faces. In fact, we pulled the car over to the side of the road and just wept there together. But these were not tears of joy over Griffen's adoption, though we were certainly joyous about that. Rather, they were tears of joy over *our* adoption into God's family. In that moment, we were given a new insight into exactly what God the Father had done for us through salvation. Though we did nothing to deserve His favor, He gave us a new name and entitled us to all the rights and privileges of His "natural child," Jesus Christ. What a powerful realization!

"But when the fullness of time had come, God sent forth His Son, born of woman, born under the law, to redeem those who were under the law, so that we might receive adoption as sons. And because you are sons, God has sent the Spirit of his Son into our hearts, crying, 'Abba! Father!' So you are no longer a slave, but a son, and if a son, then an heir through God" (Gal. 4:4-7).

God taught me so very much about Himself through Griffen's adoption! Possessing a deep love for music, I attempted to put my thoughts on paper and to write a song dedicated to my new baby boy. With both sides of our family present in Indiana once again for the Thanksgiving holiday, we all sang it together at Griffen's baby dedication service on November 26, 2006.

YOU NUMBERED ALL MY DAYS

From the very start of time You knew what I would be;
You formed each tiny inward part, then knit my destiny.
My frame could not be hidden, though in secret it was made.
Before I even saw the world, Your purposes were laid.

Chorus:
You numbered all my days before I knew a one.
You had a special plan for me before life had begun.
I'll trust Your perfect path for me and praise You for Your ways;
You made me just the way You planned, then numbered all my days.

Creator of the universe, of things both great and small,
You care enough to count my tears and watch the sparrow fall.
You number every tiny hair and weigh the deepest sea.
Why should I ever question how much You care for me?[4]

As I think back to that moment one Sunday morning when I knelt before God and submitted my dreams and desires to Him, I am struck with a renewed confidence in His goodness. He had such a good plan for my life all along! One that would bring me such joy and satisfaction. Imagine all the blessings I would have missed out on entirely if I had not submitted to Him! Blessings that far exceeded any pregnancy. I cannot accurately express in words the joy of knowing that God used me to be a direct agent of His grace toward another human being. That His eternal redemptive plan for Griffen included me! That because of His great love, He stepped outside the natural family cycles to accomplish the supernatural.

Beyond that, I gained greater insight into my salvation. I understand more deeply what it really means to be a child of God. I appreciate more fully all the rights and privileges that accompany my redemption. Plus, I have a daily, physical reminder of God's grace right in my living room and a tangible reminder that God's ways are always best!

> *"For my thoughts are not your thoughts, neither are your ways my ways, declares the LORD. For as the heavens are higher than the earth, so are my ways higher than your ways, and my thoughts than your thoughts"* (Isa. 55:8-9).

* * *

King David was referenced in the previous chapter as one who learned to wait on God. Though anointed as a young boy to be the future king of Israel, God spent many years preparing him for the task before finally fulfilling His promise. With more Scripture dedicated to this man than to any other Old Testament character, the lessons to be gleaned from his life are endless. David is found in sixty-six chapters of the Old Testament and fifty-nine places in the New Testament. He was the youngest son of Jesse, and his very name means "beloved."

In the New Testament, King David was memorialized as a man after God's own heart who followed all His will (Acts 13:22). From early on in his life, he demonstrated complete faith in the God of Israel when, as a young boy, he confidently stood before the giant, Goliath (1 Sam. 17). David possessed a deep love and adoration for God's laws, spending much time meditating on their truths (Psa. 119:47-48). Even after falling prey to the great sins of adultery and murder, David demonstrated genuine sorrow and repentance (Psa. 51:1-2). His heart of devotion to Jehovah God can be clearly seen in the seventy-three psalms that he authored.

Humanly speaking, if anyone deserved to have their prayers answered and their desires met, it was David. It was he who penned the very words, "Delight yourself in the LORD, and he will give you the desires of your heart" (Psa. 37:4). Inspired by God Himself, David confidently affirmed that the righteous desires of the God-delighter would be fulfilled. And yet, even *this* David faced unfulfilled righteous desires.

Many years before David's reign, God made an unconditional covenant with Abraham to give a specific land to his descendants (Gen. 15:18-21). After the passing of many generations, Joshua was the nation's leader upon Israel's monumental entry into the Promised Land. God had given him very clear orders to utterly destroy all the heathen nations within the borders of Canaan (Deut. 7:2). These wicked people groups lived in hatred and rebellion toward God, and their very existence posed the potential to rapidly spread their immorality throughout the nation of Israel. But in Psalm 106:34, it was recorded that the people "did not destroy the peoples, as the LORD commanded them." As a result, God was angry and handed Israel over to her enemies (Psa. 106:40-41).

By the time David finally became king, the nation of Israel had been dwelling in the land of Canaan for 440 years. But due to their disobedience, they had never fully enjoyed the territory the way that God had intended. Instead, they lived in constant subjection to their enemies. Throughout the reign of King David, however, God worked mightily to bring down many of Israel's long-time opponents.

David continually sought the direction of the Lord as he led his army against each enemy nation. He prayed regularly and acquired God's approval before each battle (2 Sam. 5:19). As David obeyed God's instructions, many nations were defeated under His power. In Second Samuel eight, David was named God's agent in subduing the Philistines, Moabites, Arameans,

Ammonites, Amalekites, and King Hadadezer. He accomplished all of this because "the Lord gave victory to David wherever he went" (2 Sam. 8:6, 14). And David quickly acknowledged God's might in all his success. He wrote, "Through *your* name we tread down those who rise against us" (Psalm 44:5b—emphasis mine).

Probably his greatest military success, however, was the defeat of Jerusalem, located in the very heart of this Jewish country. It had remained unconquered for over four centuries of Israel's existence in the land and was both inhabited and heavily defended by the Jebusites. Seven years into his reign, David decided to take on this political giant. Despite being considered a secure and impenetrable city, David's men cunningly gained entry through a water shaft and brought down this central power. This miraculous victory led to the worldwide recognition that David was a serious political force. After moving the capital of Israel to Jerusalem, his kingdom and palace were erected. Jerusalem became known as the City of David, and he reigned from this location for another thirty-three years.

As David obeyed God and followed His direction in conquering these many heathen nations, his earthly throne was established. An elaborate palace was built for him right in the heart of Jerusalem, and he dwelt comfortably within its grandeur. But as he looked around at the majesty of his surroundings, he was struck with the realization that his mighty God, Who had empowered all his success, still dwelt within a flimsy tent. For many years, the ark of the covenant made its home inside the temporal and unimpressive fabric of the ever-moving tabernacle. Recognizing that God deserved so much better, it became David's great desire to build a more permanent and elaborate home for Yahweh. He wanted the surrounding nations to recognize the One responsible for all the great victories in Israel.

Can you imagine a more righteous desire than this? To build God a temple that would magnify His great name. To showcase His glory and give worth to His worship. To make Him shine among the surrounding nations.

And yet, despite this righteous desire from one who walked in obedience to God, David was denied its fulfillment. In First Chronicles 22:8b-10 God instructed David, "You shall not build a house to my name, because you have shed so much blood before me on the earth. Behold, a son shall be born to you who shall be a man of rest. I will give him rest from all his surrounding enemies. For his name shall be Solomon, and I will give peace and quiet to Israel in his days. He shall build a house for my name . . . "

At first glance, it would seem that David was being punished for being a man of war. But as we have just established, it was by God's very instruction that he was a man of bloodshed. David had walked in obedience to God as he destroyed nation after heathen nation. So, denying his request was not a punishment.

Then why was such a request denied? Because God had different and higher plans—plans beyond anything David could have ever imagined! God desired to honor David even further and bestow even greater blessings upon him (1 Chron. 17:18-19). While David wanted to build a house for God, God wanted to build a house for David. In an unconditional covenant to His beloved servant, God declared, "Your throne shall be established forever" (2 Sam. 7:16b). God desired to build a permanent dynasty of kings on which a Son of David would rule forever. And how interesting to note that this very dynasty *required* David to be a man of war and bloodshed.

As we are able now to consider the entirety of Scripture, we gain greater insight into God's eternal plan. Jesus Christ, the ultimate Son of David, brought fulfillment to this promise of so many years before. While a complete and literal fulfillment is yet to be revealed for the nation of Israel, Jesus' death on the cross established a spiritual kingdom that will never be destroyed. While David possessed but a shortsighted view for bringing God glory in the present, God possessed an eternal and redemptive view which extended into eternity. God was at work to establish an eternal throne that brought redemption for all of mankind.

And how did this man after God's own heart respond to the denial of his desires? " . . . Do as you have spoken . . . your name will be magnified forever . . . " (2 Sam. 7:25-26). He wholeheartedly submitted and recognized that God would satisfy his earthly desires in a different and better way. And in the end, David found even greater courage to pray (2 Sam. 7:27).

So many of these lessons learned can also be applied to my own life. While my deep desires for a pregnancy were natural and righteous, God clearly had different plans for me—bigger and better plans. While it may never be fully comprehended on this Earth, I have gained a small measure of insight. My desires were shortsighted and temporal. But God's desires were eternal and lasting. He desired to use my life as an extension of His grace. He desired to offer redemption to another helpless human soul. He desired to widen my vision far beyond the simple confines of my own little, personal view. He desired to transform my understanding of His salvation for me and to teach me vividly of His great love. And He desired that I be happy and fulfilled walking in *His* ways.

Friend, you *must* come to that place in life where you recognize that God's ways are truly best! Your eyes can see only the little speck of time right in front of you. But He sees a picture of all eternity. His plans are working all things together for our good and His glory. They are better than anything you think you desire or need. They will bring you more fulfillment and joy than anything you can imagine. They will usher in eternal blessings. As you plead with God to answer some desire of your heart, pause to consider if He might be desiring something different. Something bigger. Something better. Sometimes, God is simply waiting for your submission!

CHAPTER FIVE

SOMETIMES GOD FORTIFIES MY FAITH

"And will not God give justice to his elect, who cry to him day and night? Will he delay long over them? I tell you, he will give justice to them speedily. Nevertheless, when the Son of Man comes, will he find faith on earth"

(Lk. 18:7-8).

SO VERY MANY OF OUR dreams were realized with the addition of Griffen into our family. Our hearts just overflowed with love and pride for this little person who instantly captured our world. I glowed with satisfaction as I meandered through the baby aisle of any given store—a place I finally belonged. Mother's Day became a celebration of much joy instead of a dreaded day of sorrow and longing. And even the simple daily routine of life brought so much pride and purpose.

I quickly embraced the beauty of adoption. Any fears or hesitations I previously possessed soon vanished. While my desires for pregnancy still existed, I was also very eager to begin the adoption process a second time. Even before Griffen's first birthday, we had already contacted Baptist Children's Home and started working toward completing another adoption home study. We knew that the normal process could take many months or even years to complete, and we greatly desired to have a sibling close in age to Griffen. So, our motivation was strong to get things moving.

We completed our background checks and updated our adoption scrapbooks and paperwork by early summer of 2007. We faithfully set aside money each month to fund this second endeavor, and our hearts eagerly awaited God's guidance. Above all, we prayed fervently and faithfully for God's sovereign direction toward the very child He desired for our home. And our hearts eagerly anticipated His leading.

But in September of 2007, our lives changed drastically. In an instant, we learned that our time in Berne, Indiana, was over. Rob's employment suddenly ended, and a mere six weeks remained at this ministry. God had empowered us to serve in this location for three-and-a-half years. Though difficult, He taught us much about love, sacrifice, and submission. God used the conflicts and criticisms to grow our faith and increase our endurance. We had often sensed His pleading to persevere and to learn to love even our "enemies" (Matt. 5:44). But while we had remained out of obedience to God, a sense of relief accompanied the news that our time in Indiana was now over.

Rob sensed the great pressure to provide for our little family and immediately started preparing resumés and making phone calls to churches around the country. Several contacts arose in Florida and Pennsylvania; however, conversations soon revealed that they were not the right fit. Within a matter of weeks, however, God miraculously directed our steps to Calvary Baptist Church in Derby, Kansas. This church had searched unsuccessfully for a music pastor for over a year. But from the very first conversation with the senior pastor, we gained hope that this, indeed, might be the place of God's leading. Rob filled out many pages of information and spent hours on the phone interviewing with the pulpit committee. At every single turn, it seemed that he was in total harmony with the leadership in all areas of doctrine, ministry, and vision.

After two busy weekend visits, plus the completion of the candidacy process and the church voting procedures, Calvary Baptist Church extended Rob the official offer of full-time music director, with other pastoral and counseling duties on the side. In many ways, this was the dream job that he had long desired. This relatively large church ministry provided music opportunities that seemed limitless, and Rob's interest in biblical counseling ministries grew. And so, employment in Indiana ceased at the end of September; and two weeks later, we unloaded the moving truck in Wichita, Kansas. Due to a gracious severance package, we never missed even a single paycheck. God provided abundantly for every need, and we were extremely grateful!

We knew that selling our house in Indiana might take some time and accepted that double house payments were inevitable. So, we placed most of our belongings into a storage unit and signed a temporary lease on the cheapest apartment that we found in the area. In fact, thinking that this was going to be only a short-term dwelling, we agreed to the terms of a lease before even seeing the place. We confidently asserted our ability to live anywhere for a few short months. And so, upon our arrival, we simply tried to overlook the many carpet stains, the rickety front staircase, the crumbling back balcony, and the overwhelming stench of smoke in the unit. After all, our focus pointed toward building new relationships within the church, and this housing arrangement was only . . . temporary.

But month after long month passed by without any news from our Indiana realtor. Despite now paying the mortgage, utilities, and maintenance on a beautiful home that sat completely empty, we went many months at a time without even a single showing. And the flaws in our current living condition intensified. One evening as we sat down for dinner, we looked out the back window to see our neighbor's second-floor balcony lying broken on the ground below. As the seasons changed, we felt the cold breezes blow right through our not-so-airtight home. And the *piece de resistance* proved to be the live mouse, who made his unwelcome appearance several times before frantically and permanently being trapped inside the wall. In the end, the process of selling our house in Indiana lasted more than five years, and the temporary nature of this apartment extended well beyond our expectations.

Finances were very tight, and we both felt the daily pressures. Beyond the housing expenses, our previous two-income status also ceased with the move. I taught private piano lessons part-time in Indiana, which brought some additional income to the family. But now our piano sat unused in a dark storage unit, and my financial contributions ended.

When shopping for groceries, my calculator added up each item that I placed in the cart as I purposed to stick to the food budget. Rob biked to work more frequently as he attempted to save money in the gas budget. We removed anything frivolous from our expenditures, and the monthly contributions to our adoption savings account halted abruptly.

Also during this time, I once again started to experience serious problems with my eyes. Even before we unpacked all of our boxes in the apartment, my vision deteriorated to a place that deemed me legally blind. This drastic change left me unable to read or drive and brought about a sudden and unwelcome dependence on others.

My contributions to church ministry suffered greatly as a result of my poor eyesight. I struggled to read music, which left me severely handicapped to play the piano or sing specials. What had once been my greatest joy and service to the church was now seriously hindered and difficult. Desperately wanting to find my place among this new congregation and to prove that I had something to offer, I endeavored to participate. I spent many hours at home holding music two inches from my face as I tried to memorize the notes and lyrics on the page. Then I prayed that my memory would hold up enough to perform. But despite almost perfect grades while earning my bachelor's degree in music education, plus my many years of musical experience, it was usually I who sang the wrong musical note or entered the song at the wrong measure. I experienced continual humbling, and my inadequacies were clearly evident. My former confidence vanished and ushered in a newfound fear as I worried about my ability to even find my place on the stage. I now counted the number of stairs up to the platform and practiced walking to the pulpit. No one in my new hometown of Derby knew my true potential. No one knew my past abilities. No one understood the contributions I desperately longed to make.

My other passions in life included home decorating, scrapbooking, and entertaining company. However, those also became nearly impossible for me to enjoy. We had no home of our own and little money to decorate. Because of my eyesight, working on my digital scrapbooking projects became difficult, and the space to entertain was limited. Cooking also posed a real challenge, and most everything took longer than expected. During one particular period of time, I questioned why the lunchtime sandwiches I prepared for Griffen and myself were consistently so chewy. That is, until I finally realized my failure to remove the paper wrappers from the cheese slices. If I struggled to fix lunch for a two-year-old, then how was I to manage hosting dinner parties for guests?

On top of all this, our new church family consisted of more than five hundred faces that I couldn't see. Meeting and remembering people proved extremely challenging. My normally confident personality was now quite shaken and insecure. On one occasion, a family invited us out to eat at a local soup and salad bar. Hating to be so totally dependent, I cautiously attempted to walk through the buffet line all by myself, though I had little idea about what I placed on my plate. To say the least, I ate one very interesting plate of "salad" that day. And while I possessed the ability to find humor in such situations, these regular incidents ushered in a feeling of timidity and fear. I worried about bumping people in the hallways or tripping over obstacles I failed to see. While Rob arrived in the sunflower state of Kansas with eagerness to embark on a new adventure, I showed up an invalid, unable to contribute much of anything at all.

Those early months after the big move were painfully difficult for me. I will never forget the day that I glanced across our small apartment living room and experienced the crushing realization that I was unable to clearly see Griffen's face. I can vividly remember the scene—my toddler in a striped, gray sweater against a white backdrop. Yet, no amount of effort brought his image into focus. The tears poured as I thought about a future in which I no longer remembered the features of his precious face or no longer possessed the ability to watch him grow up.

Yet despite this handicap, I desperately wanted another baby. A sibling for our now two-year-old son. Another child to complete our home and add a much-needed spark of joy. A sense of purpose in this place of uselessness. While I possessed limitations, I believed that I was fully capable of caring for the needs of a newborn. My willpower and determination propelled me to work through my obstacles, and my can-do spirit was convinced that I was qualified. In many ways, my desires for a second child exceeded those of the first. I knew how much love and happiness abounded with the arrival of our firstborn and needed another ray of sunshine in this dark existence.

Our hopes of achieving natural pregnancy still existed, even with the passing of our sixth wedding anniversary. But month after month, we continued to be disappointed. We hoped for another adoption placement, but knew of the many obstacles to that dream as well. We feared that our meager adoption savings were insufficient. We worried that our less-than-ideal living conditions held the potential to turn birth parents away from our profile. And we wondered if my eye problems posed an added deterrent. Little by little, discouragement set in as I turned my attention away from God's faithfulness and started to believe Satan's lie that God no longer cared about my situation.

My whole life, people had told me that I possessed a gift with children. I was the babysitter whom kids requested. I was the children's worker who captivated and held the attention of young faces. And with a younger sister who excelled above me in just about everything else, I clung to the hope that motherhood offered the opportunity for me to shine. I believed it was my gift. My calling. My purpose. Beyond that, it was my greatest desire. Yet, these expectations that I had for my life remained unfulfilled. When my body refused to function and adoption seemed like a faraway dream, I was crushed.

I must insert here that I am normally a positive, upbeat, and happy person by nature. Those who know me well do not view me as easily discouraged, sensitive, or emotional. I feel compelled to say this because, by its very nature, this book serves to highlight some of my darkest earthly moments. Moments that have driven me to my knees. Moments that have found me pleading for the mercy of a loving God. And it has been those moments that have preceded my life's greatest victories. It has been those moments that have inspired the very fabric of this book. And so, by necessity, they must be included. But in those dark and lonely moments of life, my normal smile was replaced with countless tears. My normally stable façade became wearied by doubt and disappointment. And my confidence in God soon questioned if this compassionate Being really cared about my life. About my desires. About me.

Then August, 2008, rolled around, and the one-year anniversary of our move to Kansas approached. I faithfully practiced a song on the piano that I was scheduled to play during the Sunday morning offering on the twenty-fourth of that month. Though it required a tremendous amount of extra work to learn the music with my limited eyesight, I viewed it as an act of my personal worship to God. When such opportunities arose, I tried to choose a song that really reflected the present cry of my heart. I wanted my musical offerings to be genuine and knew that God received glory even in my expressions of weakness. "Does Jesus Care?" by Frank E. Graeff proved to be the easy choice that month.

> *Does Jesus care when my heart is pained*
> *Too deeply for mirth and song,*
> *As the burdens press,*
> *And the cares distress,*
> *And the way grows weary and long?*

The tears streamed down my face as I sang aloud with the piano. It was the honest cry of my heart. I wondered if Jesus really cared about me. As the music swelled into the chorus, I sang even louder, determined to convince myself of its truth.

> *Oh yes, He cares, I know He cares,*
> *His heart is touched with my grief;*
> *When the days are weary,*
> *The long nights dreary,*
> *I know my Savior cares.*

I longed to experience His care in a tangible way. I desired to feel His loving arms around me and to hear His voice of compassion in my ear. As I practiced over and over again, hunched inches away from the music on my electric keyboard in the small, run-down apartment we called home, I desperately wanted the faith to believe that this Jesus remembered me.

Then after many weeks of such weariness, He acted. On August 23, 2008, just one day before my scheduled offertory, this One Whose care I doubted reached down from the glory of Heaven and gently touched me. In a single, Sovereign moment, my life changed forever. In His omniscience, He enacted a plan destined to teach me eternal lessons about His deep care and compassion.

It was a Saturday afternoon, and the 2008 Summer Olympics were in full swing. Griffen napped quietly in his bedroom, while Rob and I settled comfortably onto our sofa to watch the USA versus Spain gold medal basketball game. (To this day, my husband assures me that this was the greatest Olympic basketball championship in all of history.) As the teams began their warm-ups around four o'clock p.m., I received a call on my cell phone. Despite an unfamiliar number, I answered.

The voice on the other end began, "Good afternoon. I know you don't know who I am, but I am calling you from Adoption Advantage, a Christian adoption agency in Tennessee. There was a baby boy who was born this morning in Memphis, and we do not currently have any adop-tive families for him. I was given your number because I heard that you might be interested."

This was an agency we had never heard of before. We wondered how they even acquired our contact information—an unsolved mystery to this day. A totally unexpected call on an uneventful day.

Despite the questions, my heart soared with excitement as I jotted down information on a small piece of scrap paper—"Baby Boy. Healthy. Memphis, TN. Available for immediate adoption placement." The agent asked me a series of questions about our current home study and eligibility. My anticipation grew with each minute that we talked.

She continued, "Well, if you want him, he's yours. I will send you the hos-pital information, and we can have an agent meet you there at his discharge."

Then, just when I thought my heart was about to explode with joy, she concluded, "All you need to do is bring a copy of your home study and $29,000."

Instantly, my heart sank, and time seemed to stand completely still. There was no way we had that kind of money! We had about only $10,000 reserved for an adoption and had long feared that amount would be insufficient. We also knew from experience that there would be expenses even above and beyond the $29,000 placement fee. Another interstate adoption meant addi-tional travel costs and several weeks of hotel living. We still owned a house that refused to sell, and we knew that just the addition of a second child posed a strain on our finances. Even beyond all this, the agency required the money immediately. There was absolutely no time for fundraisers or loan ap-plications. It was a Saturday afternoon, and the banks were closed. No matter how much we wanted this tiny baby boy, this mountain seemed impossible to overcome.

I sadly expressed to the adoption agent that, despite our intense desire, there was just no way that we possessed that kind of money right now. I began to say goodbye to this one who held my very dreams in her hands. This wasn't about our willingness. It was about our ability. And we clearly were not able.

But just before I officially ended the phone call, Rob emphatically gestured in my direction. In a loud whisper he asked, "Aren't we even going to pray about it?" Now my poor husband had heard only one side of the conversation, so maybe he missed the part about the $29,000. Always the dreamer and visionary, he was surely unaware of the logistics. And the realization that this commitment required us to get up off that couch and change the entire course of our life immediately failed to sink in. Whether just trying to be submissive or simply desiring to hold on to any small glimmer of hope, I cautiously followed his advice and asked the agent for a minute to discuss the matter with my husband.

Now, it must be noted that I grew up with the king of fiscal conservatism. My whole childhood, my father preached that debt was totally unacceptable. Aside from our home mortgage, we never even considered a loan of any kind. Even in these times of great financial pressure, we committed to living within our means.

In our marriage, I am the saver, the planner, and the voice of restraint and reason. I am the one who preaches stewardship and faithfulness "in the unrighteous wealth" (Lk. 16:11). I manage all our family finances and strive to "count the cost" before making any big decisions (Lk. 14:28). So, in my very logical mind, I knew that this adoption made no financial sense whatsoever.

Rob, on the other hand, is the free spirit. He is the one who more easily can just step out in faith. He delights in sitting back and watching God provide. Money is of little interest to him, and he spends little time worrying about the future. He gives to those in need with little concern for personal cost. He is "generous and ready to share" (1 Tim. 6:18). In truth, he is the perfect balance to me.

Maybe you are beginning to see what a real struggle this potential adoption posed—a genuine test of my faith. My mind quickly argued both sides of the case. On the one hand, God dropped this opportunity onto the scene aside from any pursuit or striving. This baby was potentially the answer to almost two years of faithful prayers. I knew that God was more than capable of providing for this adoption fee, and there was no question whatsoever that this precious little soul was worth the expense. But even if the possibility existed of borrowing this money immediately, it meant saddling ourselves to substantial debt right in the midst of our current financial needs. It meant turning our backs on every ounce of reason and logic. And it meant going against everything I knew about stewardship and wisdom.

Looking back, I am so thankful for the wise leadership of my husband that Saturday afternoon. Holding hands, we knelt by our couch together and prayed. We asked God to give us supernatural wisdom and direction. We pleaded for insight to know the perfect balance between stewardship and faith. And we asked Him to make abundantly clear His ways, His path, and His will.

Then, recognizing that in the multitude of counselors there is wisdom (Prov. 15:22), we made a few phone calls. Rob went into our bedroom and called his dad, while I remained in the living room and called mine. Truthfully, we prepared ourselves to follow whatever direction these godly advisers pointed us toward.

Ironically, after giving my dad all the details of the situation, he asked for a minute to pray about it himself—a request that came as no surprise. But in truth, I expected the return call to be filled with concern and hesitation. To be a gentle dose of reality, reminding us of our current financial situation. To be the voice of reason, encouraging us to wait for God to bring along an adoption that we could afford. In my heart of hearts, I believed that the end of this irrational dream was soon to come through my dad's wise counsel.

After several minutes, Rob emerged back into the living room to express the full support of his parents toward whatever decision we made. This reaction also came as no surprise. They were generally slow to offer any specific advice for our life, and they recognized the magnitude of this decision. They understood both sides of the argument and trusted us to follow what we believed to be right.

Finally, my dad's return call came at the height of anxious anticipation. Little did he know then, but the fate of our family rested almost entirely in his wise counsel. His reply surprised me more than anyone. "Heidi, your mom and I think that you guys should do this. It is simply too miraculous. We can wire you the money immediately, and you can pay us back over time."

Just like that, in one single moment, our lives changed forever. With the support from both sets of parents, Rob made one final phone call to our pastor. Our employer. Our shepherd. Our friend. Despite the fact that we had numerous responsibilities for the very next day in church and that we offered no return date from this adventure, he also showed overwhelming support.

We quickly packed several suitcases, gathered the pages of our adoption home study, awoke Griffen from his nap, loaded up our car, locked our apartment, made a quick stop by our cramped storage unit to retrieve our infant car seat and a box of baby clothes, and then began the eight-and-a-half-hour drive to Memphis, Tennessee.

While the excitement was tangible, the fears were also present. This was a tremendous test of my faith! Logically, it made no sense at all. Though living through the greatest financial pressures we had yet known, we were about to empty all of our savings and add debt. There was no end in sight to the double house payments. The value of our only car fluctuated greatly with the amount of gasoline currently in the tank. And at one point in the drive, I glanced through the check register to see if we even had enough gas money to make it to Tennessee and back. Yet despite it all, we believed strongly that this was God's perfect will for our family. And so, in an act of great faith, we followed His leading.

As we drove late into the night that Saturday evening, we sporadically looked at each other and asked, "Are we really doing this?" After a small amount of sleep at a hotel, we continued to drive much of the next day. During those exciting hours in the car, we made numerous phone calls to share our big news with friends and family. We also settled on a name for this newest member of our family.

Our precious son, Rhys Aaron Fuller, entered this world just after midnight on August 23, 2008, weighing five pounds, ten ounces. We received that momentous phone call at four o'clock p.m.; and by seven p.m., we began the drive to Tennessee. We arrived in Memphis on Sunday afternoon and secured a hotel for several days. Then we found a Walmart where we purchased some diapers, formula, and a tiny, striped, blue and brown outfit for him to leave the hospital in. By Monday morning, the paperwork was all ready, and we received details on where and when to meet our adoption agent at the hospital.

Torrential rains poured down outside as we ran into the large, inner-city medical complex. After walking past an armed guard, we took the elevator up to the neonatal floor. As we stood outside the newborn nursery, we strained to look through the bars of the window and tried to guess which baby was ours. But with all the heavy security, there was only one small sliver of glass through which to see. We took turns as we watched the nurses lift him from his crib and dress him in the little outfit we had purchased the day before.

Then after several moments, our adoption agent, Carrie, emerged from behind the locked doors holding our tiny son. There was no drama. There was no fanfare. There were no birth parents. There was just our new little family of four all together at last—three of whom were smiling brilliantly from ear to ear.

Our love for Rhys was immense, and the bond was immediate! Having been through the adoption process already once before, nothing at all felt more natural. There were no fears or insecurities this time around. There were no doubts about our decision. Plain and simple—this little boy was ours. And we were his.

Once again, God scripted exactly what He knew was best. Rhys was born to a thirty-seven-year old, divorced mother of two teenagers, named Tina. She was not entirely positive of the identity of the birth father, but believed him to be a construction worker with whom she had had a one-night stand. She failed to remember the name of this individual and was completely unaware of her pregnancy until just one week before delivery. Consequently, she received no prenatal care whatsoever; and despite her small, athletic frame, she kept this baby a secret from almost everyone. After delivering him at an estimated thirty-four weeks gestation, Tina left the hospital before we even arrived. She called an agency and expressed her desire to place him for adoption with a Christian family. Tina never saw our photo album or read our adoption profile. She never knew about our meager apartment, current financial pressures, or physical limitations. She never desired to meet us or to have any future contact. She signed away her parental rights because she knew that this precious baby boy deserved to be in a stable home with two involved parents who wanted and loved him. And for that, we are eternally grateful and forever hold Miss Tina in high regard!

This new little life seemed to fit flawlessly into our family. Rob and I often stood back and marveled that God had given us *two* little boys! Griffen quickly adored his new baby brother and the sight of them together brought abundant joy. My heart overflowed with gratitude for God's goodness and the genuine care He showed for my life.

Almost immediately, we watched God provide. We needed to remain in Tennessee for the interstate adoption compact to be completed and knew from experience that this process could extend for several weeks. Within a matter of days, God provided for all of our housing needs. After hearing our story, a Christian family in the area gave us the keys to their large, beautiful home and offered free lodging for as long as necessary. They recently moved and awaited the sale of their house. While most of the property was empty, a dining set, a bedroom set, functioning appliances, and other smaller items remained. The residence showcased a gorgeous, fenced-in yard and positioned itself near a walking trail and park. Another Christian stranger arranged for a television to be delivered for our entertainment; and with the summer Olympics in full swing, we greatly appreciated this kindness. A handful of toys and a backyard sprinkler also offered much amusement for our two-year old bundle of energy. In the end, our time in Tennessee lasted for eighteen days, and our lodging expenses were almost nothing.

God continued to provide for our other needs as well. We met a random stranger at the public library one day who delivered baby clothes and other miscellaneous items after casually asking about our baby. The owners of a quaint, little donut shop also showed kindness when they offered Rob a quiet place to sit and work each day. And as an added bonus, they sent him home with free donuts each afternoon.

Several surprise visitors helped to make our eighteen-day waiting period in Tennessee pass by quickly. That very first weekend, my parents came to meet their newest grandson and spoiled us with restaurants and special outings. A tour of Graceland, visits to the park, and swimming at their hotel happily filled our days together. Also memorable was an evening visit from some former church friends, who drove several hours just to congratulate us and to take us out for pizza.

When we finally received the green light to return to Kansas, we excitedly loaded our car and headed home with full hearts. Upon our arrival, a clean apartment, a warm dinner, and blue streamers and balloons welcomed us. Throughout the next few weeks, church families continued to gift us with meals and boxes of clothes and even surprised us with a baby shower one Sunday night after church. What a joy it was to introduce Rhys to our church family and to feel their overwhelming love and support!

But God's goodness continued to abound. One Sunday morning in September, just weeks after Rhys' birth, our pastor pulled us aside before the worship service to inform us of another miracle. That week, the church received an anonymous donation in the amount of $10,000 allocated toward our adoption expenses. After combining this generous gift with several other smaller donations we received, plus adding our personal adoption savings and an early withdrawal from an IRA investment, we watched our debt disappear. In just six weeks, God provided for every penny of Rhys' adoption!

God taught us so much about faith throughout this whirlwind adventure! He taught us about His big plans for our lives. He reminded us again of our need to follow His eternal vision and His sovereign plan. He showed us the benefits of stepping outside our comfort zone to accomplish His perfect will. And He abundantly demonstrated His power and ability to provide.

"We ought always to give thanks to God for you, brothers, as is right, because your faith is growing abundantly . . . " (2 Thess. 1:3).

* * *

Sometimes, God answers prayer with a test of faith. Nowhere is this demonstrated more clearly than with the nation of Israel. Over and over again, needs arose; prayers for deliverance were offered; God intervened; Israel forgot the Source of her blessings; sin entered; more problems arose. In Judges six through eight, they found themselves once again doing "evil in the sight of the LORD" (6:1). As a result, God gave them over to the hand of the Midianites, who oppressed them for seven years. Each harvest season, this nomadic enemy descended upon the fields of the Israelites and stole their crops, completely devastating the nation's agriculture and food supply.

Once again in desperation, "the people of Israel cried out for help to the Lord" (6:6). And once again, God faithfully answered. He responded with one of the most iconic of all Old Testament stories—one of the greatest tests of faith in all history.

God appointed Gideon as the agent of Israel's deliverance, then instructed him to gather an army. This battalion of thirty-two thousand men paled in comparison to the 135,000 Midianites encamped at the foot of the hill of Moreh. Yet, "The Lord said to Gideon, 'The people with you are too many . . .'" (7:2). At God's instruction, Gideon told all who were fearful to go home, and twenty-two thousand men returned.

Once again, God said, "The people are still too many . . . " (7:4). Upon further instruction, Gideon eliminated ninety-seven hundred more soldiers who knelt by the river to drink water. The odds were now stacked at humanly impossible levels—135,000 Midianites versus three hundred Israelites.

But there was more. Next, God revealed His weapons of choice as mere trumpets, empty jars, and torches of fire (7:16). The leader of this rag-tag looking group of men doubted more than anyone (7:9-11).

At ten o'clock p.m.,[5] just after the Midianites changed guards in the night watch, Gideon signaled action. The Israelite army blew their trumpets, broke their jars, and shouted loudly. The Midianites were so disoriented and confused that they turned on each other as the Israelites watched from safety around the camp. In this epic battle with themselves, 120,000 Midianite soldiers died (8:10). "So Midian was subdued before the people of Israel, and they raised their heads no more. And the land had rest forty years in the days of Gideon" (8:28).

Nothing about this mission seemed logical. In fact, it appeared to be the picture of foolishness. Yet, *this* was the plan that God ordained. A plan that showcased His salvation. A plan that glorified His name.

There are many other such examples throughout Scripture of individuals whose faith was tested. In a world full of evil, "Noah found favor in the eyes of the LORD" (Gen. 6:8). The instructions? Build an ark approximately 1,518,000-cubit feet large and weighing about 43,300 tons on dry land away from all water sources (Gen. 6:13-21). The purpose? To obliterate wickedness from the face of the earth via a worldwide flood. The test? Do you really believe I can do *this*?

While no exact numbers are recorded in Scripture, it is believed that Noah worked faithfully between fifty-five to seventy-five years building this ark.[6] In Second Peter 2:5, this man of favor is labeled as a "herald of righteousness," yet he experienced no conversions throughout his ministry. Dedicating much of one's life to building a massive boat on dry land while preaching to mocking onlookers must have seemed absurd. But in a world where evil was normal, Noah obeyed God, "and became an heir of the righteousness that comes by faith" (Heb. 11:7).

Other such examples of God developing faith in the lives of believers abound. As we move to the New Testament and study the call of the disciples, we see Jesus' instructions to Peter, Andrew, James, and John (Matt. 4:18-22). The test? Walk away from established careers. Forsake family responsibilities. Leave comfort. Come now. Yet, despite leaving stability to follow a stranger, Christ calls them followers, not foolish. Such accounts remind us that sometimes God's ways defy human logic. Sometimes, they require immediate action. Sometimes, they drastically alter one's course in life.

Biblical truths about stewardship and wisdom still remain at the forefront of my mind. Such principles still guide much of my life. I recognize that each and every situation is unique and that blind faith is not the answer for all of them. Yet, as a result of Rhys' adoption, my faith is fortified.

Sometimes, God answers prayer with a test. Sometimes, He desires that I decline my own discernment. Sometimes, He wants me to reject all human reason. Sometimes, He wants me to leap without looking back. Sometimes, He wants me to stop everything I'm doing and drive, without directions, to a baby that's been abandoned in a hospital far from home, trusting a messenger I've never met and committing to a cost that's inconceivable. Sometimes, He just wants my faith! May the sincere prayer of our hearts be like that of the apostles in Luke 17:5, "Lord, 'Increase our faith!'"

CHAPTER SIX

SOMETIMES THE SAVIOR IS SUFFICIENT

"A thorn was given me in the flesh . . . Three times I pleaded with the Lord
about this, that it should leave me. But he said to me, 'My grace is sufficient
for you, for my power is made perfect in weakness.' Therefore I will boast all
the more gladly of my weaknesses, so that the power of Christ may rest upon
me" (2 Cor. 12:7b-9).

ADDING RHYS TO OUR FAMILY brought such a sense of completeness. Such joy. Such hope for the future. His presence made our apartment seem brighter and the financial pressures seem fewer. There was never a single instance in which we doubted our decision—a statement holding great significance considering what happened next.

As we settled into our new routine back home in Kansas, our efforts turned toward finalizing Rhys' adoption. We were told that this process could be completed in as little as two months . . . but that was not to be our story.

Just weeks after Rhys was born, our agency, Adoption Advantage, was shut down by the FBI for fraud. They were found to have scammed countless couples out of thousands of dollars in adoption fees. After receiving our check for $29,000—a fee intended to be all-inclusive from placement to finalization—they ceased work on our case. Despite numerous phone calls and messages, contact with this agency abruptly ended. With its founders now in prison and our adoption still not finalized, we were forced to hire additional lawyers in both Tennessee and Kansas to proceed with our case. The costs now crept upward to about $33,000 and the hassle of the process lasted an entire year. At one point, I asked our lawyer if we should press charges against the agency for not fulfilling their end of the contract. The answer? They owed more money than all the insurance companies in the world could hope to repay and that the story for most of the poor families involved did not end with a baby. We decided to count our blessings and to walk away.

Now, I was over the moon in love with our newest addition, but all the injustice and frustration involved with his adoption really caused me to think. There was no question about the fact that Rhys' adoption was costly. In fact, it came at a very high price. But First Corinthians 6:20 reminded me that I, too, was "bought with a price." And my adoption into God's family cost abundantly more than anything we had endured.

As I meditated on that truth, I penned the lyrics to this song which I dedicated to my new son.

THE PRICE HE PAID FOR ME

Why did the Author of the ages come to live on mortal land?
Why did He trade in robes of majesty to hold His mother's hand?
Why would the Maker of the universe be born a peasant's birth?
Why did He give up Heaven's glory for a simple carpenter's worth?

Why did the Omniscient give up authority?
Why did the Omnipotent surrender willingly?
Why did the Creator permit such mockery?
He could have called down fire, but instead chose agony.

Why did One so innocent take beatings for a crime?
Why did He let the mockers watch Him fall up Calvary's climb?

Why did blood so freely flow from guiltless, nail-pierced hands?
Why did the Almighty God permit such cruel demands?

But as I sat and gazed at my precious newborn son, it all became so obvious. The chorus provided the answer to all these questions.

Because there was no price too high to pay for me,
He would do anything that I His child might be.
Though I may never comprehend His sacrifice,
I know I'm His because my Father paid the price.[7]

From the moment I held Rhys in my arms for the first time, any cost seemed insignificant. Why? Because he was not expensive—he was priceless. And as I meditated on God's love for me, I gained new understanding into His heart—a heart with similar feelings toward me.

There were so many times in those early weeks and months after Rhys' birth that I just stared at my boys and thought, "I can't believe God gave me two of them!" I felt so immeasurably blessed. My heart overflowed. My life epitomized the words of Proverbs 13:12, "Hope deferred makes the heart sick, but a desire fulfilled is a tree of life."

God also graciously brought a measure of healing to my eyes. Though permanently blinded in my right eye at the age of sixteen, several minor surgeries restored the vision in my left eye to about 20/25. This was some of the best eyesight I had ever experienced. I reveled in the ability to distinguish leaves on the trees again and even gained the ability to function without contacts or glasses for the first time in my life.

Our housing situation also improved. While our home in Indiana took more than five years to eventually sell, we were blessed with several different sets of renters throughout that time. Our finances improved tremendously by this fairly stable monthly income. And on May 1, 2009, we moved out of our tiny apartment and purchased a beautiful home in a quiet sub-division across the street from a park.

Life was very good! We thoroughly enjoyed this season of blessing in both our personal and ministerial lives. I excitedly began furnishing and decorating our new home. I became more and more active in our church—playing the piano for choir, special music, and offertories. During this time, my side of the family also came together to form a music publication and performance ministry called Forever Be Sure. My sister and I had developed a real passion for writing music, and this new endeavor really served as an outlet for this love. We formed a ladies' quartet and established an annual ten-day ladies' tour each spring. This proved to be an amazing time of sweet, Christian fellowship and added opportunities to serve the Lord. Yes, life was very good.

I wholeheartedly enjoyed my role as a wife, mother, and Christian servant. My prayers shouted faithful praise and thanksgiving. My lips testified regularly of God's goodness. And if I had been able to live in a bubble, void of outside interaction, such happiness and satisfaction would likely have continued for a very long time.

But as I existed in this blissful stage for which I had long yearned, my focus slowly shifted away from God's goodness and began to compare my life with those around me. Most of my friends also had young children at home. Many continued to add to their families. And one thing I learned rather quickly was that my story was very different.

A typical church function usually found the men on one side of the room, while the ladies congregated on the other side. And the typical conversation among my female peers generally turned to family and children. Ladies talked endlessly about their pregnancies. They relayed countless details about their food cravings, sonograms, and birth plans. Those who had recently given birth relayed the whole experience—from the moment their water broke until the moment their baby entered the world. And when those little ones joined such gatherings, discussions centered around how much each child resembled his or her parents.

Now, I was a proud and joyous mother of two little adopted boys. I delighted in sharing my experience, as well. And, as is true for most people, I genuinely believed my story to be the most interesting and unique of them all. But as I gushed proudly about the gift of adoption in my life and openly shared the intimate details, I soon learned that most friends simply could not relate. Uninformed comments shattered the belief that I finally belonged in the "mom club." Thoughtless words silenced my praise and diminished God's work in my life. And hurtful statements turned tears of joy into those of great pain once again.

"Do you know his real parents?"

"Are you prepared to help him cope with the trauma of adoption?"

"What are you going to do the first time he gets mad and says you're not his real mom?"

"I could never adopt. It would be like taking food away from my own kids."

"I would rather never have kids than to take someone else's baby."

"My friend has three children. Two are hers, and one is adopted."

"Blood is thicker than water."

"You could never have the same bond with your adopted children that they naturally have with their biological mother. Even the Bible references the tie a nursing mother has with her own offspring."

Now, here I was. I had grieved. I had submitted. I had followed God's plan. And after years of longing, I had experienced great joy. Yet just when I thought my pain was erased and my desires were fulfilled, I was brutally confronted with the fact that I was still different. That I still did not belong.

For the record, I do not believe most comments are vindictive. I do not think their intentions are to bring me pain. People talk about what they know and understand. And my story is unique and unknown to most.

The purpose of this book is *not* to educate about adoption. It is not to teach proper adoption etiquette. It is not even to promote adoption as a worthy cause to pursue. The purpose of this book is simply to highlight God's guidance in my life and to showcase its sanctifying power along my journey.

However, I sincerely believe that a proper understanding about adoption is essential to understanding salvation. So, please allow this brief rabbit trail, and take it for what it's worth. The following misconceptions about adoption can pose great risk of hurting others, hindering effective ministry, and most of all, diminishing the work of Christ at Calvary.

Adoptions are born out of difficult and, most often, sinful life situations. (Fornication, adultery, rape, criminal activity, etc.) It is rare that a loving and stable couple just decides to place their baby for adoption.

Sin hurts! When a person chooses to live contrary to the ways of God, there are painful consequences. Those consequences affect the lives of many around them, including their children.

Adoption is the Providential rescue of a child by God from these natural effects of sin. For reasons we may never understand, He reaches down in love and supernaturally spares them.

Adoption provides a *better* life for the child. I do not say this to insinuate that adoptive parents somehow possess an extra measure of virtue. I say this because it is truth. In our modern Western culture, couples are screened and evaluated extensively before being able to adopt. At the bare minimum, our laws require financial and mental stability, a safe residence, and an absence of criminal activity. Beyond that, an adoptive parent *wants* the child. Do not miss this truth—adoption provides a *better* life!

Adoptive parents sacrifice much to adopt a child. The financial expense, emotional turmoil, and legal processes are daunting. An emphasis of pity toward the birth parents tends to devalue the genuine act of love by the adoptive parents.

Blood is *not* thicker than water! In fact, marriage is the closest human union ever designed by God—a relationship not of blood. Equally deep bonds can exist between parents and their adopted children.

Adoptive parents are the "real" parents. Adoption is the very real and legal transfer of a family's name, genealogy, and inheritance to one not naturally deserving of such benefits.

If God desires, you can adopt, too. His power accompanies His leading.

Not all adopted kids are traumatized. Some learn to reject Satan's lies that they really belong somewhere else—that their life is incomplete. Some grow to recognize the truth of God's immeasurable goodness in rescuing them from a tragic situation. Some understand adoption as the unmerited position of honor that it is.

This is the picture of adoption for every child of God! *This* is the imagery He uses throughout Scripture! *This* is the thinking that is imperative in understanding salvation! God rescues sinners from the tragic consequence of sin. He offers a beautiful new existence—complete with a new name, a new genealogy, and a new inheritance. God desires a deep and intimate relationship with His children. And He delights when His children look gratefully forward, rather than longingly back.

Now that I have clearly described my deep, personal feelings about adoption, it must also be noted that, at times, I myself have allowed Satan's lies to creep into my thinking. I have allowed the comments of others to take my focus away from the many good things that have been given to me and toward the things that have been withheld. And specifically, during this particular period in my life, I turned my attention away from God's eternal work and toward the temporary nature of my existence. Slowly, but surely, my exuberance faded, and I noticed anew that I still existed in a category all alone.

In my fairly large circle of friends and acquaintances, there were no other adoptive moms at that time. None. None who had endured the long road of infertility. None who had experienced the miracle of adoption. None who understood the capacity to pour every ounce of your dreams and desires into a child not gifted through blood. And as the years passed, even the handful of my friends who eventually adopted were also blessed with biological children. Children by blood. Children like them. Children "of their own."

Oh, how Satan loves to get us to believe the lie that we are all alone! That no one understands us. That we are different. That there is something missing from our present. He relishes in twisting the truth that God's blessings are not enough to bring us happiness. He is actively working to deceive each one of us and delights to take our focus away from God's Sovereign and good plans.

In my life, the devil focused on the areas of infertility and adoption. He wanted me to believe that I was broken. Incomplete. That God's greatest blessings toward me were only second best. He wanted to turn my focus away from all the gifts that God had given and toward all the things He had not. He wanted me to feel alone and unaccepted. And little by little, I allowed it to work.

While I adored my two little boys, I once again prayed for a biological child. Such prayers weren't driven so much by a desire for more kids as much as a desire to find acceptance in the eyes of others. In my mind, I could only ever be considered a "real" mom if I experienced pregnancy. I also believed a natural child to be the proof I needed that both adopted and biological children could be equally loved. I somehow concluded that my life was intended to prove this to the world.

In 2009, we once again considered fertility assistance. Friends occasionally offered advice or strategies that worked for them. One minor procedure in particular seemed to fit our situation. After discussing it with my doctor, an appointment was scheduled at the hospital. This cost-effective and rather non-evasive strategy ensured that my ovarian tubes were open, while coating the inside of my uterus with an oil to enhance implantation. Thus, in the seventh year of our marriage, we upped our efforts to conceive naturally once again. But just as before, month after month passed by without any success.

My regular menstrual cycles had always been difficult. The abdominal cramps often paralyzed and usually extended from my chest to my knees. I regularly laid helpless in bed until they passed and depended heavily on over-the-counter medications and heating pads. At times, the pain was so intense that vomiting accompanied it. But such discomfort had existed from the very beginning. I failed to know anything different. I wrongly assumed that this was normal.

In December of 2009, I was scheduled to participate in our church's annual Christmas vespers service. I had numerous musical responsibilities that could not be neglected. But the very day of this program, my monthly period arrived with a vengeance. I laid in bed and writhed in pain. I cried and cried, unable to even move. But beyond that, I frantically stressed about the fact that somehow, I needed to get to church that night and perform. I cranked the heating pad to its highest setting until the skin across my abdomen was scorched. I swallowed ibuprofen like candy—one after the next—until I had consumed about eight or nine pills. When no relief seemed to come, I took some Vicodin, which remained in our medicine cabinet from a previous surgery. As the pain intensified, the vomiting arrived. This ugly ordeal lasted for several long hours, until finally the muscle cramps subsided, and the welcomed relief finally came.

After the program that evening, I relayed my eventful afternoon to a friend and expressed how thankful I was to even be present that night. I affirmed that this was all just part of my natural menstrual cycle and again stated how lucky men are to avoid such ordeals. But as we talked, her face turned from casual interest to concern, as she said, "Heidi, that is not normal. You need to see a doctor."

It had never really occurred to me that what I experienced was any different from any other woman. But as I studied the issue further in the weeks ahead, I learned that I had every possible symptom listed for endometriosis—a condition that my OB/GYN had suspected for about a year. I had ignored her warnings and viewed them as merely possible explanations for our infertility. But the more I read, the more I realized the serious symptoms that often accompanied this untreated disease.

After another appointment to discuss my concerns, a laparoscopic surgery was scheduled. During the procedure, our theories were confirmed when endometriosis was discovered all throughout my abdomen. After its removal, tests verified that my ovarian tubes were open and that our chances of pregnancy were now significantly increased. Following several months of recovery, our hearts soared with anticipation as we once again tried to conceive.

But the year 2010 slowly turned into 2011. Our efforts resulted in twelve disappointing months. And while the surgery had substantially reduced my pain, my infertility still remained.

Nine years into our marriage and I *still* wrestled with this discouragement. How desperately I longed to be transported past this stage of life! How badly I wanted to just accept the fact that pregnancy may, indeed, never come to our family! How much I desired to find joy in God's blessings and to find victory in my pain!

As the seasons continued to change, this became the topic of many of my prayers. And as the prayers continued to flow, the requests continued to change. I found myself now bargaining with God. If He determined that a pregnancy was not best for me, then I longed for my loneliness to be removed. I prayed that He would bring along one friend into my life who related to my story. I longed for just one friend who understood the pain of infertility. One friend who knew the right words to say. One friend who had experienced the blessing of adoption. One friend who shared both my pain and my joy. And then, one day, God answered my prayers!

At our church, there were three full-time pastors—the senior pastor, the youth pastor, and the music pastor. Our senior pastor, Kent Holcomb, was a faithful and kind leader of almost forty years in this same ministry. Then in 2007, within five months of each other, Caleb Bowman and my husband, Rob, were hired on as the youth and music pastors respectively. These three men had a wonderful working relationship and possessed a deep love and respect for each other. And the wives shared similar friendships.

After working closely together for several years and growing in our relationships, one day, Caleb and Amie Bowman confided that after several years of infertility themselves, they had begun the process of adoption. They had recently undergone a series of fertility tests and had received the news that they would likely never get pregnant. And so, after much consideration, they turned their attention toward adoption.

I was *so* excited! God had answered my prayer. And I could not have picked a more perfect candidate than Amie to fulfill the longings of my heart. We worked closely together in ministry. We shared a love and passion for God. And since our extended families lived many hours away from us, our relationship as members of the same church body went much deeper than mere friendship. We were family!

My mind raced with ideas of how to protect and help Amie on her adoption journey. I immediately began to dream of hosting a huge baby shower. And I praised God wholeheartedly for meeting me personally with such kindness and pity.

I basked in the joy of answered prayer for several weeks, until one spring day I received a phone call from Amie. She asked if she could come by my house later for a short visit. A bit unusual, I wondered if maybe she had some exciting adoption news to share. Maybe they had even been placed with a baby already. I eagerly awaited her arrival.

A short time later, we were seated across from each other in my living room. Without hesitation, Amie announced, "We just found out we're pregnant." My heart sank as she continued, "We were so shocked. We were totally prepared to adopt, but God decided to give us a baby of our own." There would be no more adoption.

Everything within me wanted to run sobbing into my bathroom. But how selfish was that? Amie had also endured the pain of infertility for several years and had now been met with an answer to her own prayers. I loved her family and desired her happiness. But her happiness required my pain.

My heart was crushed. God had heard my lonely cries. He knew the desires of my soul. And He answered! He blessed me with a friend who finally understood and who could walk this sparse road with me.

But as the words, "a baby of our own," fell off of Amie's lips, I knew that a vivid chasm separated our two worlds. She would never fully understand the beauty of adoption. My dream could not be recovered. Once again, I was alone.

My husband listened regularly to my cries. He listened as I poured out my heart and bore the depths of my soul. He listened to my grief and feelings of loneliness. He listened. And listened. And listened.

And one evening in particular, as we sat across from each other at our kitchen table, he counseled me. He tenderly looked in my eyes. He compassionately held my hands. He wisely pointed me toward Scripture. And there were two things that night which really stood out.

First, he challenged me to consider if God wanted me to stop praying for a pregnancy. He pointed me to Second Corinthians 12, where the apostle Paul discussed a certain "thorn in the flesh" he dealt with. Though few details are recorded, it was likely some type of a physical affliction. Something he disliked. Something about his life that he wanted to change. Something he begged God to remove. "Three times I pleaded with the Lord about this, that it should leave me," he said in verse eight.

Paul believed his life would be improved and his ministry more effective if God took away his thorn. So, three different times he prayed for deliverance. But his fourth, fifth, sixth, or seventh prayers are not recorded. No indication is given that he continued to seek relief for the remainder of his life. Nothing points to him being consumed with this handicap. No, Paul prayed three times, and then he stopped.

The second truth my husband challenged me with that night in our home is revealed in God's answer to Paul's prayer in verse nine: " . . . My grace is sufficient for you, for my power is made perfect in weakness . . . " As this verse is studied more deeply, it is learned that the word "grace" is derived from the Greek word *charis,* and can literally be interpreted as pleasure, joy, and favor bestowed by God. The word "sufficient" is derived from the Greek word *arkeo,* meaning "to be possessed of unfailing strength; to be strong, to suffice, to be enough; to be satisfied, to be contented."[8] This verse could literally be interpreted, "God's favor (*charis*) is enough (*arkeo*) to bring you total satisfaction."

These verses brought such conviction to me! Like Paul, I falsely believed that my life would be more complete and my ministry more effective if only I experienced a pregnancy. Unlike Paul, I was consumed with this desire as I prayed for my "thorn" to be removed on countless occasions. The quiet night that I knelt by my bed and committed to God that I would never again request a pregnancy is forever etched on my mind. And by His grace, to this day I have fulfilled that promise.

God desired to teach Paul that He was enough. It was not part of His perfect plan to remove Paul's thorn. The many favors He had already bestowed were more than sufficient to satisfy.

Oh, how powerfully these truths applied to my life! God had blessed me abundantly already. He had shown Himself mighty time and time again. And these many tokens of His grace were enough to bring complete contentment. Beyond that, even apart from these many blessings, God Himself was enough to fully satisfy.

As Rob and I sat together that night, he looked at me and said, "Have you considered that 'alone' might be God's desired place for you?" An uncharted path. A desolate road. An existence rarely understood by others.

He further suggested that God may have chosen this loneliness for me in order that my complete satisfaction could be found in Him alone. As the fog of Satan's lies slowly cleared, I realized that fulfillment would never have followed a pregnancy. Comfort would never have come through an earthly friend. Relief would not have resulted from relationships.

* * *

"In YOUR presence there is fullness of joy; at YOUR right hand are pleasures forevermore" (Psa. 16:11—emphasis mine).

"The afflicted shall eat and be satisfied; those who seek HIM shall praise the LORD . . . " (Psa. 22:26—emphasis mine).

"[The LORD] satisfies you with good so that your youth is renewed like the eagle's" (Psa. 103:5).

"For HE satisfies the longing soul, and the hungry soul HE fills with good things" (Psa. 107:9—emphasis mine).

"YOU open your hand; YOU satisfy the desire of every living thing. The Lord is righteous in all his ways and kind in all his works" (Psa. 145:16-17—emphasis mine).

These words "satisfy" and "fullness of joy" in the verses listed above were translated from the original Hebrew word *saba*, a word used in ninety-two different verses throughout the Old Testament. In *Strong's Concordance, saba* is described as a verb, meaning "[to] have enough; [to] be full; [to] have plenty of; [to] satisfy; [to] suffice; [to] be weary of."[9] Can you imagine such abundant satisfaction? Through *saba,* the power of Almighty God is highlighted.

In Psalm twenty-three, we are also reminded of God's tenderness. There, He is pictured as a kind and loving Shepherd. In verse one, David declared, "The Lord is my shepherd; **I shall not want**" (emphasis mine). He knew that under God's care, he lacked nothing. All his needs disappeared. All his wants diminished.

But beyond the simple provisions for His flock, the Shepherd described here went far beyond the bestowment of basic needs. He anointed heads with oil. Literally, He fattened. He made prosperous. He satisfied. Such goodness not only saturated the flock, but also overflowed in abundance.

Through His goodness once again, I slowly realized that God was enough! No earthly friend or confidant would ever hold a candle to the tender heart of such a Shepherd! He wanted my aloneness so that my completeness could be found in Him.

Friend, please do not believe the lies of the devil. Do not fall into the trap of his deception. He desires to isolate and depress, while God offers complete contentment, fellowship, and satisfaction.

This is not a feeling that comes naturally. It takes active work to focus on truth! Some truths that I must continue to focus on are the following:

My situation is not unique to me.

"Is there a thing of which it is said, 'See, this is new'? It has been already in the ages before us" (Eccl. 1:10).

Wisdom offers grace toward the insensitivities of others.

"Do not take to heart all the things that people say, lest you hear your servant cursing you. Your heart knows that many times you yourself have cursed others" (Eccl. 7:21-22).

Comparing myself to others is not wise.

"But when they measure themselves by one another and compare themselves with one another, they are without understanding" (2 Cor. 10:12b).

God intimately knows my deepest feelings.

"I will rejoice and be glad in your steadfast love, because you have seen my affliction; you have known the distress of my soul" (Psa. 31:7).

Jesus is a wonderful Friend!

"A man of many companions may come to ruin, but there is a friend who sticks closer than a brother" (Prov. 18:24).

God's Word is truth! So, fill your mind with Scripture. Surround yourself with those who love it. Cast down the lies of the devil. Actively work to renew your mind.

As you desperately plead for some desire of your heart, prayerfully consider if God wants you to stop asking. To stop striving. To stop looking for fulfillment in all the wrong places. To rest.

Nothing of this world will ever truly satisfy! Nothing. No pregnancy. No person. No power. No possession. No position. No gain.

But the Savior is abundantly sufficient! He fills to overflowing. He satisfies the deepest longing. He satiates the weary soul. And while He loves to bestow good gifts to His children, sometimes He desires to remind them that ultimate satisfaction can be found only in Him. That He is enough.

CHAPTER SEVEN

SOMETIMES GOD EXPANDS MY ENDURANCE

"Count it all joy, my brothers, when you meet trials of various kinds, for you know that the testing of your faith produces steadfastness. And let steadfastness have its full effect, that you may be perfect and complete, lacking in nothing" (Jas. 1:2-4).

A REAL SENSE OF FINALITY followed my commitment to cease from praying for a pregnancy—a real sense that our family was officially complete. A sense of stability followed, as I mentally moved past the stage of adding children and into the stage of raising them. After ten years of marriage, it certainly seemed that God had closed the door on natural conception. Plus, we had no plans to adopt again. Before Rob or I were even thirty years old, we had already spent about $40,000 on the adoption of our two boys. During the same time, we had also waved goodbye to another $30,000 loss on our house in Indiana that took more than five years to eventually sell. And while God faithfully provided for our every need along the way, such large amounts of money for such a young family proved staggering. The running joke between Rob and me used to be that unless God wanted to drop a check for $20,000 in our mailbox, our adoption journey was finished.

And then one day, that was exactly what He did.

In February, 2011, I began the process of gathering our family income tax documents once again. As a pastor's family, there were specific housing expenses that had to be collected and categorized. Beyond that, our adoption expenses could be counted as deductions and carried for up to five years. Amid all the paperwork and organization—a process I actually enjoyed—a college friend, and fellow adoptive mom, contacted me out of the blue. She explained that there had been some changes in the adoption tax credit laws that year. Previously, any adoption expenses that had already been paid could be credited against any taxes that were owed. However, in 2011, any adoption expenses not yet claimed could actually be refunded. And since adoption credits could be carried for up to five years, our unclaimed expenses for both Griffen and Rhys were eligible. At first, I thought it was too good to be true. However, several weeks later, our tax preparer confirmed that we were owed a refund of over $20,000!

Now, our two adoptions had already been completely paid for. God had provided for those, too. This refund was above and beyond! We were overjoyed with God's abundant blessing and began to strategize about how this money should be used. The ideas flooded our minds. We agreed that a substantial portion should be placed into savings, as the previous few years of financial pressures had drained such accounts. However, an upgraded car, a family vacation, and some newer furniture also made the list. This newfound freedom to consider such nonessentials proved to be a fun and exciting process.

As the list continued to grow, the conviction that we had not truly considered what God wanted us to do with these funds entered our hearts. After some discussion, we both agreed that the next week should be devoted to prayer before we settled on any financial decisions. And so, with open and submissive hearts, that was what we did.

During that same time period, Rob had been reading a powerful book, entitled *A Quest for More,* by Paul David Tripp. He brought a copy home to me and recommended that I read it, too. Its words had challenged him personally, and he had begun to use it in his church counseling ministries. And so, during the very week in which we prayed for financial wisdom, these convicting words also filled my thoughts.

> "We were placed on earth to be part of something bigger than the narrow borders of our own survival and our own little definition of happiness."[10]

> "When the enemy somehow tricks you into squeezing the size of your life to the size of your personal dreams, wants, and needs, he has got you right where he wants you."[11]

> "We get blinded to the transcendent glories of the big kingdom and actually believe that the little shadow glories of our own little kingdom are as good as it gets."[12]

> "Transcendent, big kingdom living always has the center reserved for someone other than you."[13]

> "What could be more horrible than to get everything I want and miss the one thing that I was made for? [Jesus'] death call is really an offer to a life beyond your wildest dreams . . . Shrinking your life to the size of your life is not life."[14]

Before I had even finished half of the book, I was sufficiently rebuked. My desires for financial security, vacations, and new furniture most definitely fell into the category of "little kingdom living." Such luxuries held no eternal value and accomplished no eternal goals. Suddenly, my mind was challenged to consider eternal investments that reaped eternal benefits.

Rob came home for lunch one afternoon during our week of prayer and decision-making. As we prepared our food in the kitchen that day, our conversation soon revealed that we had each individually sensed God's clear leading in regards to the use of this money. There was no doubt in either of our minds. We unanimously agreed that God had provided this money because He wanted us to adopt a third time. He wanted us to invest in another child.

A mixture of emotions accompanied this decision. Much excitement certainly followed the realization that another baby would soon be added to our family. However, a small measure of sadness also followed the realization that new furniture and vacations would not. As I sat at our kitchen table, the many scratches and dents on its surface could not be missed. I had heard it said before that belongings which endured three moves bore the same scars as those which had been through a house fire. Well, our ten-year-old furniture had been through four moves, and its deterioration was evident!

> *"As for the rich in this present age, charge them not to be haughty, nor to set their hopes on the uncertainty of riches, but on God, who richly provides us with everything to enjoy. They are to do good, to be rich in good works, to be generous and ready to share, thus storing up treasure for themselves as a good foundation for the future, so that they may take hold of that which is truly life"* (1 Tim. 6:17-19).

These verses played continually in my mind. The truth that we were rich could not be ignored. Money could not be trusted. God provided so much for us to enjoy. A "good foundation for the future" would not have resulted from a healthy retirement account. Rather, such stability followed generosity and good works. How desperately we longed to take hold of that which truly possessed life.

One Thursday afternoon, I wandered the aisles of our local grocery store. Being free of children for the day, I slowly meandered throughout each and every corner. A small clearance section eventually caught my attention. No sooner was my cart redirected, then I spotted a black kitchen table with a bright yellow sticker. While the handwritten label advertised a price reduction due to damage, it proved a substantial upgrade from our current one. Thus, for only $100, I walked out of the store that day with both a new dining table and a deeply encouraged heart. And for the next six years, I was daily reminded of God's kindness toward me—a kindness that desired both my submission and my happiness.

Our $20,000 arrived that summer; and by August, 2011, we finished our adoption home study. With funds now reserved, we eagerly awaited God's direction. Since He had led us so clearly up to this point, we also expected His clear guidance going forward.

Thus, it was no surprise when, only about six weeks later in October of 2011, we were first contacted by our adoption lawyer. The email asked if we were interested in a baby girl who had just been born in Utah. We replied with excitement and happily called our families with the news that our daughter, Moriah Grace Fuller, had just been born. Her birth date was proudly entered into the family calendar. That night, we eagerly made travel plans as we awaited further instruction. But the very next day, we were abruptly confronted with reality—a reality which extended throughout the next eighteen months of our lives. A reality in which babies were often presented for us to consider before our profile was even shown to potential birth parents. A reality in which our hearts bonded with babies who needed homes before being crushed under the realization that ours was not to be the one.

While every adoption is unique, a typical scenario begins with adoptive parents choosing an agency and becoming legally eligible to adopt. Next, they create a profile to be shown to potential birth parents, describing life in their home. When birth parents are considering adoption, they usually study numerous adoption profiles before choosing the one they like the best. Once this decision is made, it is called a match. After birth parents and adoptive parents form a match, discussions begin regarding placement, financial remuneration, and other details.

When we adopted Griffen and Rhys, we received just one phone call each time. The phone call that stated a match was already made. The exciting call that described our baby's situation and provided details for his adoption. The call that instantly grew our family and bonded our hearts to a precious new soul, who suddenly advanced from stranger to son. We soon learned, however, that this third adoption journey was to be very different from our previous experiences.

Just weeks later, Thanksgiving arrived and found us celebrating once again with both sides of our family in Ankeny, Iowa. Both sets of parents, as well as our siblings and their families, were all present. The cousins played gleefully together, while the adults reconnected. Amid all the excitement, we received a phone call from our adoption lawyer. This time, we had officially been matched with a birth mom who was just three months pregnant. After reviewing a number of profiles, she decided that she wanted us to adopt her unborn child.

Once again, we were ecstatic! The only catch—we had clearly established an adoption budget of $20,000. This was the amount that God had already provided. However, this birth mother requested "reasonable living expenses" be paid for the remainder of her pregnancy. Such fees went above and beyond the adoption fees and brought the total cost to around $27,000.

Now, this was not a new position for us, as similar financial circumstances surrounded Rhys' adoption. Remembering how richly God provided for his expenses caused us to seriously consider another leap of faith. The biggest difference, however, was that this birth mom had six months to change her mind. Six whole months of our support that would not be refunded if she decided to keep the baby in the end. She even possessed the right to change her mind about us during that time period and to choose another family. The financial risks were substantially higher.

Despite these many red flags, the emotional turmoil was real. These were real lives. Real tragedies. Real innocence. Real opportunities to affect change. And so, being singled out of the masses and chosen as the ones to reach out in tangible love toward a struggling soul and her priceless baby brought *much* to consider! Above all, we desperately feared regret. The thought of looking back on our lives someday with the realization that we failed this test was heavy on our hearts.

We spent our Thanksgiving holiday in much discussion with our family about this situation. We prayed with them. We listened to their counsel. If we had learned anything throughout our years, it was wisdom's eagerness to follow godly guidance.

After much consideration, we wrote a personal letter to the birth mom and expressed our instant love for her child. We clearly communicated our desire to proceed with this adoption. We explained our financial situation and our willingness to cover all the legal fees. However, we announced our inability to additionally cover her $7,000 in requested living expenses. While we were hopeful that her heart would be softened, we were saddened when she decided to choose another family.

We entered the Christmas season with the hope that another door would soon be opened for us. And then, as I folded laundry one Wednesday morning in December, Rob received another phone call from our adoption attorney. Our excitement soared as we heard that twins were being delivered that very day in Wichita—just thirty minutes from our home! The birth parents panicked when they suddenly learned of *two* babies, and so they immediately called our agency to create an adoption plan. They specifically asked to review family profiles of Christians in the local area. Since our lawyer believed that we were a good match, she brought our information to this couple in the hospital. For two days, we anxiously awaited their decision.

Now, this was a dream come true for me personally! I had always wanted twins. However, in a world racked with infertility and longing, such abundance seemed far from reach. I was over-the-moon excited about this possibility! Plus, local adoptions proved to be significantly less expensive and less complicated. We had traveled to different states for both Griffen and Rhys and had remained there for eighteen to twenty-eight days while the interstate compacts were completed. So, a Wichita adoption seemed like the perfect scenario. I prayed fervently. Hoped continually. Waited impatiently. But on the third day, my heart plummeted from the pinnacle of happiness when our agent announced that the couple decided to keep their babies after all.

Just days later, we were presented with a fourth adoption possibility. A baby boy had just been born in Florida. He was quite premature and was expected to spend some significant time in the NICU. His birth parents had already left the hospital and prepared an adoption plan. Since there were some uncertainties regarding his health, he was unwanted by many. We were called and asked to consider. While we inwardly hoped to adopt a baby girl, we had not limited our adoption search to a specific gender. And truthfully, we desired more than anything to follow God's leading. So from the moment we received the phone call, our hearts ached for that precious little boy. The tears fell as we pictured him lying all alone in a hospital. We informed our agent that we were interested, but expressed our inability to act for two more weeks due to some major Christmas commitments at our church. The Monday morning after our last holiday program was completed, we called back to learn that he had been placed with another loving family. Once again, it would not be us.

We had never endured this type of emotional journey before. A journey in which we were regularly exposed to tragic life situations. Situations infested with the dark consequences of sin. Consequences that harshly affected the lives of innocent babies. Babies whose futures were up for grabs and often depended on decisions made from places of instability. We deeply longed to be God's instrument of grace and rescue, but often watched powerlessly as they faded from our field of influence.

Even beyond our spiritual desires to be used by God, our longings for another baby increased greatly as we set out on the course of His leading. With each phone call, our hearts imagined *that* baby in our home. *That* baby's touch. *That* baby's cry. *That* baby's future. Yet, time after time, *that* baby disappeared while our arms remained empty.

The new year arrived with the hope that things would be different. As we neared our tenth wedding anniversary, plans ensued for a celebration cruise to the Bahamas. Arrangements were made for Griffen and Rhys to stay with their grandparents, while Rob and I looked forward to some much-needed time alone. But in May, 2012, just two weeks before our scheduled departure, we received another phone call from our adoption lawyer.

As I mowed the lawn outside that warm spring day, Rob walked over and motioned for me to stop. He had just learned about a baby girl up for adoption in Texas. She had been born very premature and was expected to have numerous physical hurdles to overcome. Several adoptive families had already been matched; however, they had walked away after seeing the severity of her condition. The call that day questioned our willingness to pursue the adoption of this fragile little girl.

Our hearts were tender as we realized again the magnitude of this decision. Not only would our anniversary cruise be canceled, but our energies might soon be turned toward the care of a potentially handicapped little girl. Beyond that, our love and finances might be poured into a child who never even left the hospital. And yet, we realized that *this* might be the perfect path that God desired. After praying together, we committed to walk through whatever doors God opened for us and acknowledged His ability to empower us for whatever road He chose.

By this point, there was only one other family being considered for this adoption. The addition of our profile gave the birth parents two choices. After a careful review of both options, they decided to choose the other family.

While I recognized that it was God who ultimately closed this door, it was still quite difficult. The truth was that we were rejected. In fact, we had now been rejected five times. Rejected from adopting unwanted babies. Rejected from taking in children with serious physical needs. Not only were we rejected by a body that failed to conceive, but now we were also being rejected by a community of individuals who desperately clamored for help. Despite the thousands of children who needed homes, we somehow failed to measure up. Failed to stand out of the crowd. Failed to be good enough.

Our anniversary trip provided some much-needed time away to relax, reconnect, and refocus. Our plane landed in Florida, where we walked the stunning beaches together. The next day, we boarded a cruise ship and reveled in the royal treatment and luxury it delivered. The food was exquisite, distinctive, and abundant. The evening shows were entertaining and comedic. The sunsets beyond the expanse of water were breathtaking. On May 25, 2012, we celebrated our tenth anniversary in high style and praised God for our years together. The boat landed at a tropical island in the Bahamas, where we spent three days at a beautiful resort. We sunbathed by the ocean, swam in the crystal-clear pools, explored the local shops, and even spent a day snorkeling in the Caribbean. This vacation was truly the refreshment that we needed.

And then, in an instant, the mood suddenly changed. As part of our discounted booking, we were required to sit through a two-hour promotional presentation. We were shuttled to another location, where lunch was provided, a video was shown, and a tour of the facility was given. After everything was finished, we were directed to sit down with one last agent, whose highest goal in life was to sell us a vacation package. And that is where things went quickly downhill.

Never had a personality changed so quickly as when we kindly expressed that we were not interested in purchasing a piece of this tropical paradise. Innocent questions about our family quickly transformed into biting accusations about our parenting. "Good parents take their kids on vacation." "Good parents invest in making lifetime memories." "Good parents make spending quality time together a priority." "Good parents desire to make their kids happy."

At any other time in my life, I would have brushed her comments away without even a second thought. However, during *this* period, such stinging remarks attacked the deepest insecurities of my soul. Maybe *this* was why God had not given me a pregnancy. Maybe *this* was why He withheld another adoption. Maybe my sorrows all resulted from my immense inadequacies. Maybe I was no good.

After leaving the promotional meeting that afternoon, uncontrollable sobs reverberated throughout our car. As we sat in the parking lot, I unleashed my every emotion. Surrounded by the vibrant colors of this tropical island, I unloaded my darkest fears.

Several days later, our vacation ended, and we sat at the airport, awaiting our final flight home. A short layover in Texas provided a few extra hours of quiet before returning to our reality. I retreated to a secluded corner of this travel hub and opened my Bible to Proverbs thirty. But while I sought encouragement, fresh tears flooded my eyes as I landed on verses fifteen and sixteen:

> *"Three things are never satisfied; four never say, 'Enough'; Sheol,*
> *the barren womb, the land never satisfied with water, and the fire that never*
> *says, 'Enough.'"*

Now, here I was. I had recently accepted that complete satisfaction could be attained in God alone. Yet, these verses clearly stated that several things "are never satisfied." And one item in particular glared back at me—"the barren womb."

I understood perfectly that the grave always accepted more dead. The ground always desired more water. The fire continually pursued greater destruction. But the barren womb? It felt as though an uncaring God nonchalantly looked down on my life and declared it unable to be satisfied. My heart ached at the image of a Heavenly Father Who seemed so unaffected by my lot in life.

We returned back home to Kansas and reentered our reality. The adoption opportunities continued to present themselves, but the doors continued to close. Despite the total submission of our finances and our family to the path of God's leading, we seemed to be met with nothing but failure.

From May of 2012 to September of 2013, I felt the greatest instability and emotional pain that I had ever experienced. I wandered helplessly through the darkest valley I had ever walked—a valley filled with the most intense emotions I had ever known. Emotions that fiercely rose to protect an innocent baby. Emotions that submitted to the new challenges each child presented. Emotions that plummeted to realize my helplessness to save. Emotions of intense longing and bitter rejection. Emotions that questioned the presence of my Heavenly Father through it all.

* * *

So far, I have closed each chapter with a beautiful new truth that I learned through each new valley of my life. However, during this particular era, I recognized none. I just wearily placed one foot in front of the other and plodded on. I saw no spiritual growth or progress. I saw no reason for my pain. I saw no purpose for this journey.

However, since time has now removed me from these difficult circumstances, the lessons I learned are exposed. The qualities that were developed are uncovered. The results that were produced are revealed. God expanded my endurance.

The Greek word *hypomone* is "the characteristic of a man who is unswerved from his deliberate purpose and his loyalty to faith and piety by even the greatest trials and sufferings."[15] It is found in thirty-two New Testament verses. *Hypomone* is steadfastness. Perseverance. Constancy. Sustaining power. Endurance. As I have since studied this biblical concept further, several truths have been highlighted.

Pain is essential to develop endurance. While one can learn to <u>wait in a</u> <u>wilderness of silence, one can learn to endure only in a valley of affliction,</u> <u>pressure, or distress.</u>

> *"Patiently endure (hypomone) the same sufferings that we suffer"* (2 Cor. 1:6).

> *"Therefore we ourselves boast about you in the churches of God for your stead-*
> *fastness (hypomone) and faith in all your persecutions and in the afflictions*
> *that you are enduring"* (2 Thess. 1:4).

> *"Looking to Jesus, the founder and perfecter of our faith, who for the joy that*
> *was set before him endured (hypomone) the cross . . . "* (Heb. 12:2).

Movement is essential to produce endurance. While waiting is the stillness of soul to rest quietly, endurance is the willful decision of the mind to move forward. When quitting seems easiest, endurance presses on.

> *"For you have need of endurance (hypomone), so that when you have done the*
> *will of God you may receive what is promised"* (Heb. 10:36).

> *"Let us run with endurance (hypomone) the race that is set before us"* (Heb. 12:1b).

> *"Pursue righteousness, godliness, faith, love, steadfastness (hypomone), gentle-*
> *ness"* (1 Tim. 6:11).

Endurance is essential to achieve full spiritual maturity. God desires the complete sanctification of every believer. The trials of life aid in producing the beautiful fruits of righteousness that lead to this lofty goal. James refers to this fruit-producing cycle as a test, and he urges believers to pass with high marks. To continue on. To remain strong. To see it to completion. Quite literally, he pleads with them to complete their test so that they may be found complete.

*"Count it all joy, my brothers, when you meet trials of various kinds, for you
know that the testing of your faith produces steadfastness (hypomone). And
let steadfastness (hypomone) have its full effect, that you may be perfect and
complete, lacking in nothing"* (Jas. 1:2-4).

*"We rejoice in our sufferings, knowing that suffering produces endurance
(hypomone), and endurance (hypomone) produces character, and character
produces hope, and hope does not put us to shame . . . "* (Rom. 5:3-5).

Rejoicing is the appropriate response. A mind that chooses to focus on the
glorious benefits of suffering can experience pure joy at their very onset—not
merely at their escape. This goes far beyond the natural tendency to merely
plod through discomfort while awaiting relief. This is the supernatural freedom to view trials as a *reason* for rejoicing. This is the ultimate power to
experience full and complete joy *because* one is learning to wait longer and
stand stronger.

*"**Count it all joy**, my brothers, **when you meet trials** of various kinds, for
you know that the testing of your faith produces steadfastness (hypomone).
And let steadfastness (hypomone) have its full effect, that you may be perfect
and complete, lacking in nothing"* (Jas. 1:2-4—emphasis mine).

*"**We rejoice in our sufferings**, knowing that suffering produces endurance
(hypomone), and endurance (hypomone) produces character, and character produces hope, and hope does not put us to shame"* (Rom. 5:3-5—emphasis mine).

These truths were not fully recognized at the time; however, much wisdom can be gleaned looking back. Though we had followed the path of God's
leading to pursue a third adoption, my heart questioned a path that failed
to produce any real results. Though we prayerfully submitted to His will, I
feared the end of a journey that failed to accomplish the goal. But while I
believed that the ultimate goal was to change the life of another child, God's

ultimate goal was to change me. During this time in my life, God faithfully produced a spirit of *hypomone* within me. He increased my ability to face suffering. He strengthened my will to press on. He developed my capacity to remain constant. He expanded my effectiveness to endure.

At first glance, this concept may seem a bit depressing. God brings trials into our life to expand our endurance so that we can face greater trials later on. He teaches perseverance in the showers, so we can weather the floods. He develops steadfastness in the heat, so we can withstand the fire. He grows constancy in the infirmities, so we can survive the valleys of death.

But when I consider those heroes of the faith who soared victoriously through the unimaginable trials of this life, I affirm the supreme value of endurance. Oh, how much I would choose stillness amid loss over fighting to retain control. I would prefer rest amid blindness over striving to preserve sight. I would embrace contentment amid bankruptcy over wrestling to gain wealth. And I would take peace amid rejection over clamoring to achieve favor. And I recognize that suffering is a necessary part in attaining such a desirable quality.

Friend, if you ever hope to arrive at this glorious place of hope and confidence, you *must learn endurance! Don't forget this truth. As you fervently lay your longings before the throne of God, remember that He is compassionately guiding you toward this beautiful end. Sometimes when you pray, God uses the opportunity to expand your endurance.*

CHAPTER EIGHT

SOMETIMES GOD SAYS NO: UNDERSTANDING THE REALITY

"And you shall remember the whole way that the Lord your God has led you these forty years in the wilderness, that he might humble you, testing you to know what was in your heart, whether you would keep his commandments or not" (Deut. 8:2).

THURSDAY FAITHFULLY PROVED TO BE the most glorious day of each week. Thursday was Rob's regular day off of work. While I adored my life as a wife and mother, Thursday broke up the monotony and fueled my excitement to continue. It was the one day each week in which I escaped the confines of my home and accomplished the family errands all by myself. On Thursday, my husband attended to all the duties at home—DIY projects, child care, cooking. Thursday was my day to personally recharge and refocus. My day to actively accomplish, rather than merely maintain. My day to move freely and without distraction. Thursday.

My regular Thursday routine included stops at the library, bank, gas station, church, Target, Dillon's, and Walmart. Often, the kids' clothing needs found me at the mall. Upcoming church events or family functions led me to the party store in north Wichita. Home repairs found me regularly at the big box improvement store. And I reveled in the weeks that provided extra time for home décor or furniture shopping. Determined to finish the list I had assembled throughout the rest of the week, I decisively moved from one location to the next.

But sandwiched in between these many gigs and groceries, I always found a quiet parking lot somewhere to eat my lunch alone in glorious peace and quiet. I enjoyed each delicious bite of food without little boys who clamored for their share. I abandoned the kid's tunes in the CD player and replaced them with the audio of my choice. I noticed the world around me and remembered a life outside of my home. And after I had leisurely finished my food, I came to the best part of all.

When each crumb was cleaned and each corner tidied, I opened my Bible and began sweet fellowship with my God. I spoke aloud to the One Who sat beside me and reconnected with the One Who knew me best. I reviewed the memory verses that empowered my daily life. I studied the Scriptures that faithfully guided my steps. I sang songs of worship that lifted my focus. And I prayed. And I prayed. And I prayed.

The most fervent prayers of my lifetime came on Thursday afternoons in my car. I spoke freely and openly with my Best Friend. I praised Him profusely and thanked Him anew. I confessed my sins and sought His forgiveness. I interceded for others and requested His grace. I poured out my longings and unveiled my soul.

Without fail, those moments alone with God proved to be the absolute highlight of my week. As we continued to face the regular disappointments that accompanied this third adoption journey, those moments each Thursday reminded me of God's supernatural leading to this path. With each new rejection, those moments encouraged me to stay the course. With each new goodbye, those moments empowered me to carry on.

During the summer of 2012, God impressed upon my heart the need to pray more specifically about this adoption. My current prayers generally asked for God's direction and sought for Him to clearly open the doors of His choosing. However, as I considered that He chose to number my hairs and count my tears, I was encouraged to also bring the unique desires of my heart before Him in prayer. As I pondered the distinct requests He had answered for others in the past, I was emboldened to tap into such mighty power personally. And so, with these truths fresh on my heart, I penned a detailed prayer list of my desires for this next adoption.

1. Financially—total cost under $10,000
2. Geographically—local, Kansas birth
3. Socially—closed adoption similar to Griffen and Rhys (contact with the birth parents severed after child placement)
4. Medically—no major health concerns
5. Promptly—placement call received after birth when birth mom could not change her mind
6. Particularly—multiples (preferably girls)

This list was not created because I expected that God *would* answer each request, but because I knew that He *could*. I feared the possibility of missing something amazing because I failed to ask. Plus, the vocalization of my specific desires brought a closeness with God and a calmness within me. With list in hand, I entered an era of the most fervent prayer I had ever experienced.

Each and every day, these requests were taken before the throne of God. I claimed God's power with each sentence. I reminded Him of His mercy, goodness, and love. I prayed direct quotes from Scripture and used specific verses to make my appeal. I eagerly anticipated an answer.

By August of 2012, some major landscaping work was being done in our backyard. Huge patches of grass, weeds, and debris were being replaced with a large concrete patio. While we hired a company to do this project, I was involved in much of the clean-up and final design. There was much heavy labor involved as I moved landscaping rock from one location to another.

In the midst of all this, my body started to experience some unusual symptoms. While my normal menstrual cycles typically came like clockwork at their appointed time each month, dark spots of blood now appeared mid-cycle. This pattern continued for several weeks. I also noticed a major swing in my hormonal patterns and changes to my normal demeanor. And in an instant, my appetite for food vanished. Nothing looked good anymore.

Truthfully, at the time, I attributed all of these symptoms to my outside labor. Sore muscles and exhaustion were also present, and the whole package seemed like a natural result of this backyard project. But as symptoms continued, concerns began to creep into my mind.

In our family, personal doctor visits were almost never scheduled. We believed that most illnesses could be cured naturally over time. Cuts and bruises could be tended at home. And the internet provided answers to most questions. However, on this occasion, fears developed that something more serious was present. Finally, I told my husband that I planned to schedule an appointment with my OB/GYN.

Now, it must be understood that after years of practice, I had learned to push aside the hopeful thoughts that I was pregnant. After so many disappointments, it took conscious effort to cast down such imaginations and to not allow myself to be consumed with symptoms. And I had succeeded to the point that pregnancy was not what I suspected now.

Yet, being the frugal financial planner that I was and knowing the approximate cost of a doctor visit, I desired to make sure that such a trip was truly necessary before committing. I theorized that the possibility of pregnancy was something that would be asked anyway. And I figured that this option should just be ruled out from the very beginning. And so, I found an expired pregnancy test in the recesses of my bathroom closet and proceeded to administer it.

A myriad of emotions overwhelmed me as I stared down at the results. The test confirmed what I had dared to believe. I was pregnant. Ten years of marriage. So much brokenness and disappointment. So much submission and growth. So much failure. So much success. With all our attention and effort focused toward adoption, this was the last thing that I expected.

I called my doctor's office and explained both the positive pregnancy test, as well as the spotty bleeding and other symptoms. The nurse comforted me with the counsel that everything could be perfectly normal. She scheduled a series of blood tests to acquire more information.

I drove to the clinic in complete awe of the whole situation. Following the first blood draw, I returned home and eagerly awaited the results. I was both shocked and overjoyed when the office called to confirm that I was, indeed, pregnant!

This pregnancy was a supernatural work of God! It wasn't a result of striving. It wasn't a result of some medical intervention. It wasn't even what I expected. I had a supreme confidence that this was God's perfect will for our family.

I needed to return to the doctor's office in two days for a second test. But those two days in between blood draws were two of the most glorious days of my life. For two days, I felt validated as a real mom. For two days, I fit in with the ladies around me. For two days, I dreamed. Dreamed of the next eight months. Dreamed of this baby's future. Dreamed of baby announcements and gender reveals. God had miraculously granted what I had ceased to request.

During those two days, Rob and I discussed making the big announcement to our family. In just a couple weeks, both sets of parents, plus Rob's grandparents, had all scheduled a weekend visit to Kansas to come and participate in Rob's pastoral ordination counsel. This was a significant milestone to be celebrated and one that we excitedly looked forward to. On top of that, Rob's thirtieth birthday was the very same weekend. With so much festivity already planned, we decided it was the perfect time to make a baby announcement, as well.

Two days later, I drove back to the clinic for my second blood draw. They desired to see increasing levels of the HCG hormone in my body. Such growth indicated a healthy and normal pregnancy.

But late in the afternoon on Friday, August 17, the clinic called with the results of my second blood test. All alone in the quiet of my bedroom, I answered the phone and listened to the emotionless voice of a nurse who simply reported the information she was tasked to deliver: "Your HCG levels dropped. You should expect a miscarriage very soon."

This tiny, seven-week-old life had answered my prayers, fulfilled my dreams, captured my thoughts, and stolen my heart. And yet on Saturday, August 18, 2012, this priceless gift was heartlessly flushed down the toilet. Instantly gone.

While this baby will forever be treasured in my heart, such loss went so much deeper than the death of my child. So much deeper than the farewell to my dream. So much deeper than the reminder of my brokenness. This miscarriage attacked the core of everything I believed about my God. It betrayed every image I possessed of a kind and loving Heavenly Father. It violated every foundation upon which I had built my world.

Just five days earlier, I had not even known about this pregnancy. I could have miscarried without any knowledge of its existence. My life would have been unaffected by this loss. God could have spared my pain, but instead He purposely chose it.

I had already abandoned this path toward pregnancy. I had relinquished my desires and followed God's path. Over time, I had come to a place of genuine trust in His good plans for my life. On top of that, I had embraced God's clear direction to adopt. I surrendered the family finances and committed to the additional costs of time and energy. I prayed fervently and walked through each open door. I loved each child that was presented and willingly considered even those with great physical needs.

And yet, how was I rewarded by this One who said He cared? No. NO. **NO**. With the "no" to multiple adoptions. With the reminder of a "no" that I had labored so long to accept. With the revival of deep wounds that I had sought so hard to bury.

I collapsed on the floor of my bathroom and just wept. Filled with anger, I clenched my fists and screamed out loud at God—a God Who suddenly appeared so vicious and cruel in nature. "How could You do this to me? How could You? How could You?" Over and over again.

The timing of everything only compounded my resentment, as our season of scheduled celebration ensued. This compassionate Being provided no time whatsoever to even grieve. It felt as though He expected me to simply get over this loss and move on with life. The very day I miscarried was also the fourth birthday party of my precious son, Rhys. The sports-themed festivities went on as scheduled. The guests arrived. The games were played. The presents were opened. But while smiles adorned the scrapbook pages, the pictures failed to capture the giant hole in my heart or the many tears that spilled out in private.

Just days later, our out-of-town guests arrived, and the celebrations continued. Things went well at the ordination, and Rob was officially installed as a pastor. A cake reception followed, and many offered their congratulations.

Next, was Rob's thirtieth birthday party. It also proceeded as planned. A delicious brunch was enjoyed on our new backyard patio, where balloons and other decorations adorned the space. Cards were read. Gifts were opened. Games were played.

That Sunday, Rob and I were scheduled to sing a joyous anthem for special music. It had been planned weeks earlier in what seemed like a different life. However, fresh pain had ushered in a wave of new emotions. That Sunday, we barely had the strength to walk in the front door of the church. We made a last-minute change in our song choice and shared a brief personal testimony about the miscarriage instead. Despite deep feelings of betrayal, anger, and confusion, we stood up together and sang this song by Rodney Griffin.

I CHOOSE

Master, may I be so honest?
Could I admit the way I feel?
I'm hurting, it seems that you've forsaken,
And I wonder, "Is your love for me still real?"
Though my friends think I'm happy,
Unaffected by this trial,
They can't see the pain I'm hiding

Just underneath my smile.
Master, I can't live this way anymore,
So today I make my choice.

I choose to believe that You are faithful
And my heart is in Your hands,
And this mystery I face today
Is part of a greater plan.
I choose not to be discouraged
When the sun will not break through.
I have the choice of trusting You.
So, Lord, this is what I choose.[16]

Our church provided overwhelming support. After the service, I was surrounded with hugs, encouragements, and prayers. Women from all walks of life shared their personal stories and offered hope for the future. Genuine, Christlike love was displayed for the weeks and months that followed.

But something else also happened that day. Every lesson I had learned along my journey was suddenly challenged. Surrounded by the well-intentioned comments of others, I was thrust instantly back to the place of desire and longing that I had diligently worked to surrender. My faith was challenged and my endurance provoked. Despite my efforts to find satisfaction in God, I was reminded again of just how alone I truly was.

"At least now you know that you can get pregnant."

"It's easiest to get pregnant again after a miscarriage."

"Keep trying. It will happen again."

This was *not* the place I wanted to be again! A place of timed intercourse and strategic moves. A place of consumed thoughts and anxious waiting. A place of continual hope and regular disappointment. I had moved past this place. Far past it. And nothing within me desired its return.

"I'm so sorry. I know this baby was the *true* desire of your heart."

"Don't worry. I know God will give you a baby *of your own* someday."

Without question, this natural pregnancy fulfilled many deep desires of my heart. However, an adopted baby would have been welcomed with equal joy. And while I grieved over the loss of my natural child, I also grieved for the six others whom, for brief moments, I had thought to be mine. As my heart ached for all of them, I realized again how few people truly understood my unique situation.

Throughout September, my HCG pregnancy levels were monitored. Each week as I drove to the clinic, my mind flooded with wonder. I wondered how old my baby was supposed to be and what developmental milestones should have been reached. I yearned for the heart that was supposed to be beating and the limbs meant to wiggle around. I considered how very differently everything was supposed to have turned out and questioned regularly my role in its departure.

Amid my despair, a miraculous ray of hope entered our world. In October, Rob was placed in contact with a pregnancy crisis center in Nebraska and was informed of another potential adoption. This group worked hard to promote life and provide support to those who faced unwanted pregnancies. A young lady, about half-way into her pregnancy with twin girls, had recently reached out to the center for help. She quickly understood her inability to raise these babies and sought guidance in preparing an adoption plan. We eagerly mailed our adoption profile and expressed our great desire for them.

Every part of my being wanted to believe that *this* was a sign of God's tenderness and healing. That this double blessing was intended to remind me of His love and pity. That God had closed one door because He had prepared something even better.

Over the next few weeks, we remained in regular contact with the head of the crisis pregnancy center. She provided consistent updates and information.

She shared our adoption profile with the birth mom and expressed our eagerness to be considered.

My hopes increased with each passing day. These girls seemed to be the answer to some very specific requests and desires. Names were discussed regularly, and several matching pink outfits were purchased. My prayers intensified as my heart yearned for these two precious lives that I desperately hoped would soon become my daughters.

But on October 27, 2012, after several short weeks of communication, we received the frantic phone call that the birth mom had suddenly faced severe preeclampsia symptoms. In her life-threatening condition, she was rushed to the hospital, and the babies were immediately delivered. At about twenty-four weeks gestation, these two little girls weighed just over one pound each. Following their birth, they were airlifted to the children's hospital in Omaha, Nebraska, and were hooked up to all manner of wires and machines.

While my heart plummeted at this news, my fierce desires and protection instincts only increased. I desperately longed to be by their side and prepared to uproot my life the very moment that permission was granted to do so. While I understood the severity of their long-term medical conditions, I wholeheartedly accepted the challenge.

The NICU staff affectionately named these tiny girls who so suddenly appeared to them Addison (Baby A) and Bailey (Baby B). They were tenderly loved and cared for. Our contact from the pregnancy crisis center also drove to the hospital to be by their side and remained faithful in her promotion of our adoption plan.

But on November 2, 2012, and November 6, 2012, each of these precious babies passed away. Their fragile bodies survived only five and nine days on this earth. Despite the lack of any legal authority, our hearts loved them as though an adoption had already been finalized.

The pain was unbearable as we spoke to the individual who unhooked each girl from her life support and held each one until her final breath. Lives we loved, but never kissed. Lives we embraced, but never held. Lives God placed in our world only to take them away.

Twice in a row now, God had presented the deep desires of my heart, only to heartlessly rip them away from me. First, it was a pregnancy. Then, twin girls—a specific request I had added to my prayer list because I still clung to the hope that my desires played some part in God's plan for my life. I included it partly as a test. With adoption calls coming regularly, I knew that the supernatural aspect of a single baby could be missed. However, I longed for a gift that came straight from the heart of my Savior. One that reminded me of His tenderness and left no question of His leading.

But this very Savior seemed to enjoy playing games with my emotions. I knew with confidence that He heard my every prayer. And He answered some very specific requests. But when He removed these gifts from my life, images of a powerful Dictator who found pleasure in taunting me with what I could never have replaced my thoughts. It seemed that He enjoyed telling me no.

Just days after the twins died, I attended Amie's baby shower at church. The room was packed with ladies who eagerly awaited the arrival of her healthy baby girl. Though surrounded by people, I felt so alone. My heart grieved a loss I had never announced. A loss I had never possessed. A loss that could not be understood by others.

These feelings of loneliness were only confirmed when I received a phone call shortly thereafter which informed me that hurtful rumors were being circulated—rumors that my infertility and miscarriage resulted from my poor sex life; rumors that accused me of stealing babies from other deserving families; rumors that I was a racist for adopting only white babies. I felt so betrayed. So humiliated. So angry. So ashamed.

"Indeed, none who wait for you shall be put to shame; they shall be ashamed who are wantonly treacherous" (Psa. 25:3).

This verse was added to my prayers as I now also pleaded for God to remove my shame. In my life to date, this was the lowest valley through which I had ever walked. In fact, the single darkest day can easily be remembered. The overwhelming feelings of loss and loneliness. The feelings that God was actively against me. The feelings that healing would never come.

And on that very day, I received another phone call. It was Susan.

Susan and I had served together for several years. We both played in the church orchestra. I accompanied her flute students on the piano from time to time. We usually sat just one row apart each Sunday morning. But even with all this regular contact, I would not have called us more than friendly acquaintances.

Truthfully, as much as I respected Susan, we possessed little in common. She was six years older than me and had never been married or had children. She still lived at home with her parents and worked full-time for her dad. She faced none of the same pressures or struggles that I did—or so I thought.

Every once in a while, amid casual conversation, Susan and I discussed meeting up for lunch sometime. However, our lives often became busy, and such an outing simply never happened. Until *that* day. On the lowest day of my life, with my swollen eyes and tear-streaked face, Susan called.

"Hey, Heidi. I was wondering if we could get together sometime this week for lunch? Do you have a day that's available?" she asked.

I very uncharacteristically responded with an answer that only accompanied my weakened emotional state. "Yeah. How about right now?"

And that is where our friendship began. Just moments later, Susan and I sat across from each other at our local Village Inn restaurant. There, at a booth in the far back corner, I sobbed through my entire story from start to finish. The years of infertility and longing. The call toward adoption. The many losses. I totally unloaded my every dark emotion.

"Where does the pastor's wife go when she doubts the goodness of God?"

"Everything in my reality clashes with my theology."

"Is my life just some kind of sick joke to God?"

"Do my desires play any role in His plans for my life?"

"Does prayer really make a difference at all?"

For two whole hours, I bore the depths of my soul to an acquaintance who is now called a dear friend. She was available. She listened. She cried. She prayed. She pointed me to the Scripture. And in the days and months that followed, she tangibly showed the love of Christ to me over and over again.

It was Susan and her mom who cooked and delivered an entire Thanksgiving feast for the family I so suddenly regretted inviting. In my season of sorrow, such celebration held little interest, and reasons to praise proved hard to identify. But the turkey and all the fixins that they prepared gently lifted my weary arms and demonstrated their sincerest support.

It was Susan who spent hours creating a large basket of gifts so uniquely designed just for me. "You have . . . put my tears in your bottle" (Psa. 56:8) was handwritten and attached with ribbon around a decorative green glass jar. Both large and small boxes of Kleenex came adorned with the words, "The Lord will wipe away tears from all faces" (Isa. 25:8), and "My soul thirsts for God" (Psa. 42:2) was paired with a drinking glass. Many other similar gifts filled the basket and, likewise, encouraged my soul. Each precious note is still preserved in the nightstand by my bed, along with the tender card that simply stated, "The last chapter has not yet been written. With Love and Prayers, Susan."

* * *

When we consider the topic of prayer throughout Scripture, we most often remember the miraculous. The healing of the sick. The defeating of the enemies. The supplying of the needs. The opening of the barren wombs. These are the accounts we cling to desperately as we come before Almighty God with our requests. Our needs. Our desires. We long to see Him be that same God to us. The God Who supplies water from the rock. Who fills the widow's jar with never-ending oil. Who supernaturally makes the leprous wounds disappear.

And we fail to consider that sometimes God says no. We don't want to believe that a loving God might sometimes choose suffering. That this compassionate Being might deem sickness best. That a path full of failure might actually be good for us.

We cherish the memory of Samuel, a man of God memorialized for his powerful prayer life (Psa. 99:6). His very existence resulted from the faithful prayers of his mother, Hannah (1 Sam. 1:27). His very name meant, "asked of God."[17] His life began under the nurture of this woman of prayer and continued in the house of prayer all the days of his life. "He was born, named, nurtured, housed, and trained in prayer, and he never departed from the way of supplication."[18]

In First Samuel seven, one of the grandest events of his life is recorded, "and yet it is fairly descriptive of his whole career. He cried, and the Lord heard."[19] The Philistines once again oppressed the Israelites, and Samuel pleaded for God's deliverance. In this instance:

> [They] marched to battle, but Jehovah went before them, in answer to the prophet's prayer. You could hear the rolling of the drums in the march of the God of armies, and see the glittering of his spear, for so is the history of the battle recorded: "And as Samuel was offering up the burnt offering, the Philistines drew near to battle against Israel: but the Lord thundered with a great thunder on that day upon the Philistines, and discomfited them; and they were smitten before Israel. And the men of Israel went out of Mizpeh, and pursued the Philistines, and smote them." The conclusion of the whole is, "So the Philistines were subdued"; that is to say, the prayer of Samuel was the conquering weapon, and Philistia crouched beneath its power.[20]

But at an old age, Samuel faced a different kind of battle that was met with very different results. After a full life devoted in service to God and the nation of Israel, the elders gathered before Samuel and requested a king like all the other nations. They desired a totally new governmental structure, which contradicted everything he promoted. Samuel knew the effects that a king would have on the people he dearly loved. Their sons would be turned into soldiers. Their daughters would be turned into slaves. Their labor would be controlled by dictators. Their profits would be taxed by the crown. With a heart full of sorrow, Samuel once again pleaded with the Lord for rescue. But this time, God said no. This time, He instructed Samuel, "Obey their voice and make them a king" (1 Sam. 8:22a).

Such a command must have perplexed the prophet. Why would the God of Israel be controlled by a sinful whim? Why would the omniscient One have sent them on a path toward such known devastation? Why would the rejection of the established theocracy be allowed? Despite a life of faithful service, such questions would never be answered in his lifetime.

As we move to the New Testament, we find great hope and encouragement as we read through the many mighty acts of God recorded in Hebrews eleven. The supernatural exit of Enoch from the earth. The rescue of Noah and his family from the worldwide flood. The conception of Isaac by his elderly parents. The preservation of Moses from genocide. The parting of the Red Sea. The conquering of Jericho. The escape from lions, fire, and sword. The revival of the dead.

But at the very end of the chapter, we also read:

> Some were tortured . . . Others suffered mocking and flogging, and even chains and imprisonment. They were stoned, they were sawn in two, they were killed with the sword. They went about in skins of sheep and goats, destitute, afflicted, mistreated . . . wandering about in deserts and mountains, and in dens and caves of the earth (verses 35b-38).

This four-verse tag at the close points us to the countless saints of God who were met with a no. Whose prayers for peace were met with the most violent torture and the most horrific death. Whose prayers for provision were met with homelessness and hunger. Whose prayers for freedom were met with captivity. Whose no's were never comprehended upon this earth.

The workings of God throughout history are unfathomable to the finite mind! The children of Israel questioned this God, Who allowed forty long years of wilderness wanderings, filled with hunger, thirst, serpents, and scorpions. The prophets of old must have questioned why this same God called them to devote entire earthly careers to eyes that would never be opened and hearts that would never be healed. And the early followers of Jesus Christ must have questioned the worth of their sacrifice as they stood at the foot of the cross.

And still today we question.

> *"Oh, the depth of the riches and wisdom and knowledge of God! How unsearchable are his judgments and how inscrutable his ways! 'For who has known the mind of the Lord, or who has been his counselor'"* (Rom. 11:33-34).

Upon this Earth, we can only ever know in part. Our imperfect eyes can see only dimly. Our simple minds can reason only like a child. But take hope. The perfect will come (1 Cor. 13:9-12). The words of Jesus to His disciples still provide confidence to each one who wonders about His ways. "What I am doing you do not understand now, but afterward you will understand" (Jn. 13:7).

Oh, what hope this offers to all generations! Someday, we will clearly see the purpose of our pain. Someday, we will comprehend the heart of a God Who always desires "to do [us] good in the end" (Deut. 8:16). Someday, we will clearly understand that when God says no, it is only because He is providing "something better" (Heb. 11:40). Something eternal. Something abundantly good.

CHAPTER NINE

SOMETIMES GOD SAYS NO: UNDERSTANDING OUR RESPONSE

"Be still, and know that I am God. I will be exalted among the nations, I will be exalted in the earth" (Psa. 46:10).

AS I CONTINUED TO PUT one foot in front of the other during this dark, spiritual valley of resistance, Susan encouraged me to start a journal. She confidently knew what I only hoped to believe—that someday this season would be ended, and my faith would be renewed. She gifted me a vintage style notebook with the words of Psalm 46:10 scrolled beautifully across the cover: "Be still and know that I am God." To this day, that journal remains one of my most treasured earthly possessions. For the next thirteen months, I recorded my every raw emotion. I wrote down the desperate prayers of my soul. And little by little, I began to see God change me. Inside the front cover were these words:

> "This journal was begun after the loss of friendships, the loss of pregnancy, and the loss of twin girls we were trying to adopt. I trust this record will document my journey out of the depths of despair to a renewed faith in a compassionate and loving God" (November, 2012).

During those first few weeks of journaling, my entries primarily begged God for compassion and tenderness. They pleaded for a Red Sea moment in which I could simply "stand firm, and see the salvation of the Lord . . . " (Exod.

14:13). I sought justice and protection from bitterness. I confessed openly and honestly my doubts, insecurities, deep sorrow, and weariness. I asked God to teach me how to pray. The many no's to my specific requests caused me to question God's desire to hear them. My mind was filled with confusion, and I longed to know truth.

In my daily Bible time, I began to study every time the word *pray* was used throughout Scripture. I wanted to know what the saints of old prayed for. I wanted to know how God responded and answered the prayers of the past. I wanted to find out which prayers God approved of and which ones He didn't.

I longed to commune with God in an excellent manner. I longed to imitate the rich prayers of my biblical heroes. And I soon realized that my current prayer life failed to measure up. This was specifically highlighted in my personal desires along this third adoption journey. On November 26, 2012, I tossed out the old prayer list and entered a new and improved one into my journal. My revised prayers now pleaded for the following:

1. To see God's miraculous power
2. To feel God's inherent compassion and tenderness
3. To experience true satisfaction and contentment
4. To have clarity of mind
5. To find acceptance and belonging
6. To know perfect peace and rest

And because biblical precedent was, indeed, found for making my personal desires "known to God" (Phil. 4:6), I included one final request at the bottom.

7. Multiple girls

While I made faithful steps of progress, the road was definitely bumpy. Days of submission and peace were usually followed shortly after by days of discouragement and unrest. On December 2, 2012, I wrote:

Lord, the best way to describe me right now is weary. I'm weary of 10-hour Sundays jam packed with service. Weary of every evening being devoted to someone else. Weary of watching others rejoice. Weary of pasting a smile on my face and pretending everything is OK. So very weary of bringing the same issues to You over and over again in prayer. Weary of waiting! Lord, I know You are in control over all things. I know that the purpose of my life is to bring glory to You. But what I do not understand is where my feelings and desires fit into that plan. I so badly want to feel the compassion You showed to Ruth, Hagar, Hannah, and Sarah. I want to see a Red Sea moment. I want my Abba Father to wipe my tears and hold me in a long embrace. I need to know that in Your quest for glory, You care when it is at my expense. I want to believe that You see the pain of a barren woman today and that in tenderness You care and long to help. I have been in the "I waited patiently for the Lord" stage for a long time now. Please hasten the "And He delivered me" phase (Psalm 40).

Four days later, on December sixth, we received yet another phone call from our adoption attorney. We had once again been matched with a birth mom who lived in Houston, Texas. Keleigh studied various profiles and had officially chosen us to adopt her healthy, ten-day-old baby girl. She had four other children (from different fathers) and was currently without any home or job. Keleigh recognized her complete inability to care for a fifth child. And so, in her desire that this child have a better life, she chose adoption; and she chose us.

Every adoption phone call came with great excitement. Since we had never embraced the concept of pursuing our own matches, each call came with the knowledge that it was supernaturally delivered by God. Such understanding brought joy and confidence to walk through the doors that He opened.

However, once again, concerns accompanied this adoption. Once again, the cost was expected to exceed $28,000—a price well above our allotted goal. Once again, this required us to completely drain our adoption savings account and dip into additional assets, as well. While we possessed the ability to cover these expenses, it was a bit discouraging to once again be placed back at ground zero.

Second, Keleigh requested that the placement not take place until January second—still four weeks away. She indicated that the adoption posed great sadness for her other four children and desired that they have the opportunity to enjoy one Christmas together before saying goodbye. And we suspected that she needed the additional tax benefits that came from having another child in her home through the close of the year.

Despite these concerns, we reluctantly obliged her request, signed the paperwork with the agency, and paid the fees in full. What really sealed our decision was the fact that a living, breathing child was already born and awaiting placement. Plus, the birth mom appeared highly committed to her decision. The additional expense seemed well worth the sacrifice for this precious baby girl, who so suddenly entered our world.

During the next four weeks of waiting, we eagerly made preparations for the arrival of our daughter. We settled on her name—Keira Ashleigh Fuller—which played off the birth mom's name (Keleigh) and the original name she had been given at birth (Cenzeigh). We rearranged our home and relocated Griffen and Rhys to a downstairs bedroom to create a nursery upstairs near our master. Splashes of pink appeared everywhere as we excitedly purchased a new car seat, new bedding, and many other newborn essentials. We eagerly filled her closet with the prettiest ruffles and transformed her room into the princess paradise she deserved.

Regular communication with Keleigh continued, and we received faithful updates and pictures of our little girl. Travel plans to be with family in Minnesota for Christmas were canceled and rerouted instead to Houston. Announcements were made. Congratulations were offered. Gifts were received.

One Sunday, just days before our departure, I sat next to Amie in the morning worship service at church. Her beautiful baby girl had just recently been born, and she glowed with all the new joys of motherhood. As I dreamed of the daughter who would soon be in my arms, several musicians got up and presented a special number before the sermon—a song based on Job 1:21. But as the words "He giveth and taketh away" fell from their lips, my heart sank. Those words so accurately described our two lives over the past year. She clearly epitomized "He giveth," while my life undoubtedly represented "He taketh away." And in those few moments, fears flooded that He would do it all over again.

As the piano played softly during the invitation at the close of the service, I gently nudged Amie and whispered, "Can we talk?" While I maintained my composure as we exited the sanctuary, the flood gates opened as we took our seats in Rob's office. Amid loud and ugly cries, I unleashed the worry that I almost dared to speak out loud: "God wouldn't dare do it again, would He? He wouldn't take her, too."

On December thirtieth, after spending a quiet Christmas alone in Kansas, we loaded up our minivan and headed south to Houston. The trunk was filled with Keira's abundant baby gear, and our hearts were filled with hope. We longed for the season of joy that seemed only footsteps away now.

Griffen and Rhys were filled with excitement as we arrived at our hotel. As soon as the car was unloaded and the room was settled, they eagerly asked if they could go swimming. With trunks on and towels in hand, Rob made one quick phone call before heading downstairs with them to the pool. He wanted to inform our adoption agent that we had arrived safely and that we anxiously awaited further instructions.

But before we had even been in our hotel room for thirty minutes, things began to unravel. Despite previous conversations regarding placement on January second, Keleigh suddenly acted shocked that we were in Texas. "I didn't tell them to come," she responded frantically. "Why are they here? We are out of town on vacation."

As communications continued, we were soon informed that our original placement date no longer worked into Keleigh's schedule. And her sudden change in personality now demanded that we give her additional money. She had already received several thousand dollars from us as part of our original agreement to cover her "reasonable living expenses." But now, she threatened that no adoption papers would be signed until we agreed to her new demands.

Keleigh's instability and deceit continued to surface. It appeared she had squandered our previous funds on a vacation with her kids. Her intentions toward adoption became highly suspicious. It soon appeared that she had played on our emotions and simply used her baby as a tool for personal financial gain. And now, this little girl was being held hostage until we agreed to pay further ransom.

We were placed in an extremely difficult and tenuous position. Keleigh's actions were strictly forbidden under U.S. law, yet the life of an innocent, little girl hung in the balance. We finally expressed our willingness to pay a small amount of additional money, but only after the adoption papers were signed and the baby was in our arms. And with that, we waited.

Rob took our boys downstairs to go swimming. In those quiet moments alone in that hotel room, I knew in my heart that it was all over. God had, indeed, taken Keira, too.

While I barely had the physical strength to even open the pages of my Bible, I honestly knew of nowhere else to turn. I had no words to even pray. I had no more tears to even cry. I had no friends who understood *this*.

In my desperation, my eyes providentially landed on Second Corinthians 4:16-18:

> "So we do not lose heart. Though our outer self is wasting away, our inner self is being renewed day by day. For this light, momentary

affliction is preparing for us an eternal weight of glory beyond all comparison, as we look not to the things that are seen but to the things that are unseen. For the things that are seen are transient, but the things that are unseen are eternal."

But rather than the intended encouragement, new sadness entered my aching heart. Is this really what God thought of my trials? Were they merely considered "light afflictions"? Were the memories of these ten babies that I loved simply transient dreams intended to be forgotten?

I had poured out my heart to God on countless occasions. He listened endlessly to the cries of my soul. And yet, time and time again, He deliberately opened doors that brought utmost joy before ruthlessly slamming them shut.

On January 3, 2013, we left Houston with empty arms. The bottom line was that God deemed it best that this precious baby girl, whom we loved, be raised apart from us. His good plans for her life included poverty instead of pleasure. Fatherlessness instead of a family. Weakness instead of warmth. Shakiness instead of stability. Immorality instead of integrity. Danger instead of dreams. Oppression instead of opportunity. Hunger instead of hope. Everything within me thought He was wrong.

God's good plans rewarded the wicked. Despite Keleigh's godless lifestyle, she won. While the adoption agency returned a portion of the fees we had already paid, her actions cost us $11,000 that would never be recovered. She flaunted her fertility when she knew our bodies failed. She played with our emotions to promote her private gain. And God allowed it. He allowed the pastor to be punished and the sinner to be satisfied.

As we drove through downtown Houston on our return trip home to Kansas, we passed by a variety of bars and adult video stores. My mind flooded with questions. "Why do the wicked prosper? Why does God allow sinners to freely enjoy everything I want? Why do I suffer so unjustly? Is righteousness really rewarded?"

We arrived home to face the empty nursery that I had so lovingly decorated. Several days later, I drove around town and returned all the baby items that had been recently purchased for a little girl I had recently loved. As I pulled into one parking space, I misjudged the distance and hit the adjacent vehicle. A long, permanent scratch all along the passenger side was instantly added to our van. It seemed that there was no end in sight!

Days later, we received yet *another* phone call. An adoptive family was needed for two month-old, boy/girl twins born locally in Wichita. They were perfectly healthy. The parental termination papers were already signed. The costs were significantly lower than anything else we had been presented. The babies were ready for an immediate placement. We were notified that our profile was to be delivered to the birth parents that afternoon.

Was permission even granted to wonder if such goodness could actually be meant for us? Would this emotional journey finally end? Would joy finally come?

With whatever strength remained in me, I sat in the empty nursery that night and prayed. And prayed. And prayed. There on that floor, I pleaded with God for mercy, while the rest of my family slept soundly in their beds. Into the early morning hours, I poured out my heart anew. I so desperately needed to see God's power displayed! I needed reminders of His love! I needed a token for good!

And once again, this was exactly what my heart had long desired. Healthy twins. Already born. Local. Immediate placement. Lower fees.

But after fiercely hoping for two days, we received the news that the twins were being placed with a different family. The nonchalant update from our adoption agency was delivered with the tone of the nightly weather report. Yet, this news was the farewell to another dream—the tearful goodbye to babies eleven and twelve.

In the days that followed, I plodded through life in utter disbelief. The year 2012 had proved excruciating, and I desperately hoped that 2013 would be different. But these new disappointments reminded me that nothing at all had changed.

One Saturday afternoon in January, I laid on my bathroom floor and just sobbed. I cried until every ounce of my physical strength was gone. It seemed like my God had totally forsaken me. It seemed like my Friend had completely betrayed. It seemed like my Father offered no assistance. It seemed like my Savior removed every hope.

After many minutes had passed, my husband cautiously peeked his head around the corner and asked, "Is there anything I can do to help?"

In rage, I shouted, "I would wish that I were dead right now, except I know where I am going when I die, and I don't want to see HIM right now!"

In those moments, I could honestly not have imagined anything worse than standing face-to-face before a God Who seemed to hate me so viciously. A God Who wielded His powers to cause me only more pain. A God Who had clearly demonstrated that He was against me.

Later, as we attempted to organize the remainder of our day that was relatively free of outside responsibilities, Rob suggested a family outing to lift our spirits. But when my reaction reflected disinterest he asked, "Well, what do you want to do?"

Looking him straight in the eyes, I responded, "I want to go sin."

Plain and simple, I wanted God to pay for all the hurt that He had caused me. Hurt that was so totally unjustified and cruel. If I was expected to suffer so endlessly, then I wanted Him to suffer, too.

My husband's response shocked me more than anything. "Me, too," he softly replied.

In that instant, I discovered the depth of *his* pain. Pain I had gravely overlooked. He was the rock. The logical perspective. The wise, biblical counselor. But suddenly, it became apparent to me that he was dealing with deep pain, too. He had also loved each one of those babies. He had also dreamed about their futures. He had also questioned God's plans. He had also possessed anger and resentment.

In the hours that followed, we loaded our family into the car and just drove. We had little care for anything at all in the world. Our emotions had gone totally numb toward a future that looked totally bleak. Honestly, we could have easily chosen any number of sins to go out and commit that evening. But looking back, God was sovereign, even in those darkest moments as He protected us from ourselves. As a Shepherd, His rod and staff guided us away from danger (Psa. 23:4). As a Mother Eagle, He spread out His wings and fluttered over us to guide us and keep us from falling (Deut. 32:11-12). The only "sin" we came up with that night was the frivolous purchase of a new, big screen television.

As I later considered the depths to which I had fallen, guilt was added to the mass of emotional turmoil within. I surmised that only the weak questioned their Creator God. Only the immature doubted His justice. Only sinners dared to be angry with Him.

In my desperation, I began to read the book of Job. There, I discovered a man who understood my feelings. A man who stated all the same things that I did, yet was considered righteous. A God-fearing man who suffered immensely for no fault of his own. A man who lost everything dear to him. A man betrayed by his friends in his time of greatest need. A man whose grief overwhelmed him to the point that he despaired of life itself.

> *"For he crushes me with a tempest and multiplies my wounds without cause; he*
> *will not let me get my breath, but fills me with bitterness . . . I loathe my life"*
> (Job 9:17-18, 21).

Job believed that God was against him (6:4). That God hated him (16:9). That God acted unjustly (19:7). Job questioned the prosperity of the wicked (21:7) and God's abandonment of the righteous (23:8). He wondered why God's goodness was replaced with cruelty (30:21).

Job demanded a day in court with God. A day in which his innocence could be proven. A day in which God answered for His vicious actions toward him. And right in the middle of Job's angry tirade against God are these words:

"Today also my complaint is bitter, my hand is heavy on account of my groaning. Oh, that I knew where I might find him, that I might come even to his seat. I would lay my case before him and fill my mouth with arguments. I would know what he would answer me, and understand what he would say to me. Would he contend with me in the greatness of his power? **No, he would pay attention to me**" (Job 23:1-6—emphasis mine).

Those last words jumped right off the page at me the first time I read them. As a mother, I envisioned a small child throwing a tantrum and angrily shouting, "It's not fair," while slamming a door in rage. And knowing my natural response to such circumstances, I marveled at the reaction of God.

In my home, such arrogance is not tolerated. Such immaturity is isolated. Such foolishness is abandoned until sin is realized and apologies are offered.

But this is not the reaction of God.

He does not demand righteousness before an appearance with Him is granted. He does not cast off the sinner until error is realized. "He does not deal with us according to our sins, nor repay us according to our iniquities" (Psa. 103:10).

No, the Creator God bends His ear to the created. He gives undivided attention to the wayward. He listens to the accusations of the weak. He extends tenderness, mercy, and love to the most unstable and rebellious who come before Him.

This image brings fresh tears to my eyes as I remember the many times I sat in my car alone and shouted out loud at Him, "You said You were good!" The times I pounded on the steering wheel with clenched fists and yelled, "These aren't the actions of a just God!" The times I raged, "Look down from heaven and see, from your holy and beautiful habitation. Where are your zeal and your might? The stirring of your inner parts and your compassion are held back from me" (Isa. 63:15).

But rather than push me aside, He listened. I wasn't resisted, confronted, or opposed by His great power and majesty. No. Just like with Job, God paid attention to me. And despite eyes that were closed to the truth, God did far more than that. He continued to provide Christian friends who took up this spiritual battle with me. He faithfully revived my spirit with Scripture. He often intro-duced music that sustained my weary soul. There were so many times that I got into my car just as the perfect song for that moment began to play.

I'LL NEVER FORSAKE YOU

By David Ward

O doubting, o fearful—remember His care,
The helpless and hopeless need never despair
For from your afflictions His glory shall spring –
The deeper your sorrow, the louder you'll sing!
Remember Your Father–His promise, His love:

"I'll never forsake you, this pain will not break you,
For I will remake you for unending joy;
My promise is faithful though now it is painful;
No power can trample my covenant love."[21]

IT PAYS TO PRAY

By Rodney Griffin

You're tempted to quit prayin'
You feel He's never listenin'
The time has come and you must make a choice
Do you stop believin'
Forget what you've been seein'
Or do you resolve that Jesus hears your voice
He will hush the angel praises
Just to hear what you are sayin'
And at any moment now you will rejoice.

It pays to pray
It pays to call upon His name
It pays to pray
To see a miracle displayed
You'll forget the word, impossible
When you seek the Savior's face
You'll know He will make a way
It pays to pray.[22]

I'VE BEEN TO THE BOTTOM

By Rodney Griffin
In sorrow I was sinking
Had all but stopped believing
Anyone would hear my call
Lost everything I treasured
Grief was beyond measure
I wondered how far I'd fall
In my desperation
I called upon my Savior
"Lead me to some solid ground."
Then, underneath the rubble
Of all my pain and trouble
You'll never believe what I found

Well, I've been to the bottom
And I've found at the bottom
There's a blessed Holy Rock
A place for us to stand
away from sinking sand

Safe in the hand of God
A foundation that is sure
and ever will endure
To comfort the hurting heart
Well, I've been to the bottom
And I've found at the bottom
There's a blessed Holy Rock.[23]

I trust that the reality has been clearly established. Creator God sometimes says no to His creation. Sometimes He deems another path best. Sometimes He uses our prayers and desires as an opportunity to sanctify. But He never abandons!

Even when God thrusts His beloved into the fire of affliction, He is there right beside them. He listens to every prayer. He pays attention to every heartache. He knows each deepest pain. And He establishes a biblical response to His sovereign verdict.

Worship and **Trust**.

* * *

In Second Samuel 12, the young child of King David became terminally sick. David fasted and prayed fervently. He laid on the ground continually for six days and begged God to spare the life of his son. However, "on the seventh day, the child died" (verse 18).

Having seen the profound effects that the illness had on the king, his servants greatly feared David's reaction over his son's death. They worried that his own suicide might be attempted due to such a great loss (verse 18). But when David understood that his son had died, "[he] arose from the earth and washed and anointed himself and changed his clothes. And he went into the house of the LORD and worshiped" (verse 20).

David possessed a beautiful understanding of the power of prayer, as he pleaded with God for mercy. However, David also understood his need to accept God's sovereign answer. Upon receiving a no, he stooped down in reverence and humbly bowed to **worship** God.

This was *not* an instant happiness and joy that suddenly appeared. This was *not* a praise fest of music and singing. This was *not* an emotional experience that transported him beyond his pain.

It may have looked like devastation. It may have been accompanied by tears. It may have sounded like confusion. It may have been filled with questions. But David's deep sorrow coexisted with abundant peace.

David's worship was an acknowledgment of God's worth. A reverential tribute to His royalty. An outward expression of His splendor. A vocal recognition of His grace.

God is glorified when we respond to His workings with worship. But worship is not the only reaction He desires. We need to look no further than the sinless life of Jesus Christ Himself.

While He knew the eternal mission of His descent to Earth, the sweat drops of blood appeared as His destiny loomed nearer. The agony that must be endured was overwhelming. Being sorrowful and troubled, He pleaded with God the Father, "If it be possible, let this cup pass from me" (Matt. 26:39). He begged God to reconsider the plan.

But even before God the Father responded with a no, the acceptable response fell from the lips of the sinless Savior. His prayer concluded, "Nevertheless, not as I will, but as you will." These words demonstrated the ultimate *trust* that Jesus had in God's better plan and a complete submission to it regardless of the personal cost.

As we are able to see clearly now, a no was necessary. Without the refusal of Jesus' request, salvation would not be possible. Suffering was required. But abundant blessings followed.

When God says no to some deep desire of your heart, it can be devastating. It becomes easy to believe the lie that He does not care. That He is not listening. That prayer has no purpose.

But God never wastes your pain. There is always a reason for your suffering. God's ways are always good, and His plans are always best. Trust the heart of your wise and loving Heavenly Father. Worship Him in your weakness. Hold on to the hope that He is working something far better.

CHAPTER TEN

SOMETIMES GOD MAKES THE MIRACULOUS: UNDERSTANDING THE REALITY

"Now to him who is able to do far more abundantly than all we ask or think,
according to the power at work within us, to him be glory in the church and in
Christ Jesus throughout all generations forever and ever. Amen" (Eph. 3:20-21).

AS WE ENTERED FEBRUARY OF 2013, a normal routine was established once again. I had cried all my tears and vented all my emotions. Our adoption savings account had dwindled to only $9,000, and we asked our attorney to contact us only if such a situation arose within the confines of this new budget. We were no longer prepared financially or emotionally for the never-ending saga that we had endured over the past many months. And from that moment on, we never received another phone call about adoption.

The busyness of a very good life began to occupy my time and attention once again. My two growing boys were now four and seven years old. In the mornings, I homeschooled Griffen and tried to keep Rhys occupied elsewhere. In the afternoons, I taught private piano lessons to ten to twelve students from the convenience of my own living room. And at church, I now accompanied for the large majority of all special music—a ministry I thoroughly enjoyed.

Over the years, Rob had developed a real passion for biblical counseling, and this soon became a large part of his service at the church. He loved to help hurting people find solutions to their problems from the Word of God. Our miscarriage and numerous adoption failures only aided his sensitivity and ability to empathize with others. Little by little, he worked on a master's degree in this field, as well as on his National Association of Nouthetic Counselors (N.A.N.C.) certification.

Part of this process included an annual trip each February to Lafayette, Indiana, where Rob attended a week-long biblical counseling conference. The teaching and encouragement he received there were invaluable to his life and ministry. And now, once again, Rob packed his suitcase, rented a car, and headed off to another week of meetings, while I stayed back and held down the fort at home.

The week proceeded just like any other. I maintained the household chores. I administered Griffen's school work. I taught afternoon piano lessons. And with the sudden lack of adult fellowship, perhaps I lingered a bit longer afterward with the mothers who appeared to claim their students. And one afternoon in particular, I bonded with one such mom, who providentially possessed the same desire for fellowship.

Being the last lesson of the day, we were not pressured by time. We were free from most distractions as our kids played happily together downstairs. And we quickly found a topic that interested us both.

I did not know Melissa or her family very well at all. They attended a different church and had a different social network of friends. Our first connection was the day she called to ask if I would teach her young daughter, Brooklyn, to play the piano—lessons she had only recently begun.

But that afternoon, as I attempted to get to know her better, questions about her family opened the door to deeper conversation. I soon learned that she and her husband had once faced infertility and that her youngest children resulted from in vitro fertilization treatments. Not only that, but embryos created from the first cycle were actually frozen and transferred several years later. I was captivated by this new realm of scientific technology I previously knew nothing about.

Her transparency made it easy for me to open up about the personal struggles we had faced throughout the past years. I briefly shared our journey and the many disappointments along the way. I ended with a statement that some things were just not meant to be.

But after finishing my personal history, Melissa said one of the craziest things I had ever heard in my entire life. One of the most insane and mind-bending statements of all time. A sentence that probably made sense only in the most outrageous science fiction movies in existence. She said, "Have you guys ever looked into embryo adoption?"

I momentarily wondered what planet she had descended from. What other whacky ideas she possessed. What other liberal concepts she embraced.

I smiled and nodded my head politely as she proceeded to explain this new-fangled procedure. A chuckle or two may or may not have escaped my lips. A worry for the future of our country may or may not have fluttered through my brain space. A small sense of relief may have accompanied her exit as I gladly welcomed the end of *this* nutty conversation.

Embryo Adoption? Just wait until Rob heard about this!

Rob returned home late Friday evening and was eager to tell me about everything he had learned. With Griffen and Rhys fast asleep in bed, he shared the many ways that the conference had lifted his spirits and prepared him for deeper ministry. A certain class designed for counseling those dealing with infertility and miscarriage proved especially rich. Rob opened his notes and shared the deep truths that were highlighted.

After many minutes, our conversation ended. The living room recliners were extended back, and we settled in to watch one television program before heading off to bed. But as we searched for a show, Rob off-handedly mentioned one more thing.

"Heidi, have you ever heard of embryo adoption?" he asked.

Well, now my interest was piqued! It was one thing to hear about this from a practical stranger. However, Rob had just returned from a biblical counseling conference filled with highly educated and devoted Christians. And now he initiated the very conversation I had found so unusual just days earlier.

Dr. Wickert was both a practicing OB/GYN and a certified biblical counselor. Dr. Wickert was also the conference teacher for the class on infertility and miscarriage. Rob was so blessed by his guidance that he remained after one session to thank him privately.

Rob briefly explained our story to him and the many discouragements we had faced along the way. He expressed our confusion over God's guidance in leading us down the many paths designed only to fail. And he thanked him for the Scripture passages that had so aptly been presented.

But before turning to leave, Dr. Wickert asked, "Have you and your wife ever considered embryo adoption?"

Like myself, Rob had never even heard of such a thing before. Like me, he thought it sounded a little crazy. And as I relayed my similar conversation with Melissa, he, too, found it a bit eerie that we both had been presented with this unusual concept in two separate venues.

The TV was suddenly turned off, and "embryo adoption" was now entered into the web browsers of our separate devices. The next hour flew by as we read article after article on the internet. In truth, the next week flew by as we continued to study much on the topic. Our shock was soon replaced with intrigue, and our intrigue soon turned to interest. Before long, we were captivated by this new realm in which one week earlier we had known nothing about.

While I do not want the science and statistics to overshadow the spiritual, this brief history will hopefully help to explain the fascinating development of embryo adoption:

In vitro fertilization is a medical procedure in which a woman's egg is removed from her body and fertilized by sperm in a laboratory. The growth and cell division of this newly created embryo is monitored for two to six days before being returned to the woman's uterus.

In 1978, the first baby conceived through in vitro fertilization was born in the U.K. As research for this brand-new reproductive technology expanded, so did its practice and success. By 1981, nine live births were reported globally, and the United States delivered its very first IVF baby.

During a typical IVF procedure, multiple embryos are created in a lab to provide the greatest opportunity for success. After being observed for several days, only the healthiest ones are transferred to the woman's body. The remainder are most often destroyed or donated to scientific research.

Throughout the 1980s, scientists experimented with the process of freezing (cryopreserving) leftover embryos. This allowed couples to save their extra created embryos for use at a later date—until the desired size of their family was achieved. On March 28, 1984, the first child from a frozen embryo transfer was born.[24]

The popularity of IVF continued to expand as new hope was now offered to many infertile couples. In 2012, U.S. doctors performed more than 165,000 in vitro fertilization cycles, which resulted in the conception of over 61,000 babies (one-and-a-half percent of total births in 2012).[25] It was also estimated that about 600,000 embryos remained frozen, awaiting the final fate of their future.[26]

Since the inception of such assisted reproductive technology (ART), millions of human embryos have been destroyed. Since the U.S. had no authoritative board over human fertilization and embryological research, there were no regulations that prohibited this practice. It has been estimated that half of all created embryos are eventually discarded. (The HFEA in the U.K. reported the destruction of over 1.7 million embryos between 1991-2012.)[27]

Throughout this medical evolution, many ethical concerns have been debated. When life actually began became a topic of much discussion. Was it at conception? Transfer to a mother's womb? First blood flow? First heart beat? Birth? Based on one's conclusion, the value and appropriate treatment of embryos was determined.

Several pro-life factions believed strongly that life began at the moment of conception and that destroying even the smallest embryo was considered murder. Rooted in this position, they sought for ways to protect and save these tiny lives, who would otherwise be destroyed. And embryo adoption was born.

Embryo adoption allowed couples to donate their remaining embryos to other families. Following a strict medical protocol, those embryos could be transferred to the body of an adoptive mother in the hopes of a successful pregnancy. In 1997, Nightlight Christian Adoptions was formed, and this option officially became available in the United States. In 1998, a baby girl named Hannah was the first adopted embryo ever to be born.[28]

At first, interest in this option grew slowly. By 2012, only eight embryo adoption agencies existed in the United States. They were primarily small, conservative, Christian organizations who held to strong prolife values. By January of 2013, almost forty-five hundred total babies had been born through embryo adoption in the U.S.[29]

As Rob and I continued our study of embryo adoption, we were especially drawn to the National Embryo Donation Center in Knoxville, Tennessee. They boldly held to strong, biblical values. Right on the home page of their website, it stated:

> While the NEDC is open to couples of all race, religion, creed, and background, our own Christian faith is the overriding principle upon which we operate. As an organization guided by our religious faith and protected by the Constitution of the United States, the NEDC firmly believes in the sanctity of life beginning

at conception and recognizes marriage as a sacred union between man and woman as defined by scriptures of the Holy Bible.[30]

The NEDC was a small, Christian, non-profit organization that held strongly to the belief that each tiny embryo was a valuable life created by God. They were committed to giving even the weakest ones a chance at life. Their top-notch staff gained national recognition for their expertise and thriving success rates. (Over fifty percent of all transfers resulted in a pregnancy.[31]) Their embryo adoption program grew exponentially each year, and they rejoiced greatly over the birth of each and every child. By the end of 2012, a total of 345 babies had been born through their embryo adoption program.[32]

As we sought to form our own personal beliefs within this ethical arena we had previously not explored, we looked to the Scripture for answers. As we wrestled with questions about the beginning of life and the entrance of the soul, it was soon established that some things will never be completely known to man. Some things were meant to remain a mystery. Some things belonged to God alone.

"The secret things belong to the Lord our God, but the things that are revealed belong to us . . . " (Deut. 29:29).

"It is the glory of God to conceal things . . . " (Prov. 25:2).

"As you do not know the way the spirit comes to the bones in the womb of a woman with child, so you do not know the work of God who makes everything" (Eccl. 11:5).

But as we continued our study, our hearts were also reminded of the great value God placed on each human life. It was confirmed that the image of God was inherently stamped on each soul. We were amazed at the thoughts and plans God determined for even the unformed embryo.

*"My frame was not hidden from you, when I was being made in secret, intricately woven in the depths of the earth. Your eyes saw my **unformed substance**; in your book were written, every one of them, the days that were formed for me, when as yet there was none of them. How precious to me are your thoughts, O God! How vast is the sum of them! If I would count them, they are more than the sand. I awake, and I am still with you"*
(Psa. 139:15-18—emphasis mine).

We soon gained confidence that God approved of those who viewed and valued life as He did. Those who cherished and protected the innocent. Those who rescued and liberated the helpless. We soon embraced embryo adoption as a noble and worthy endeavor upon which God smiled.

As we sought guidance to determine if God had called *us* to this good path, the answer was quickly and clearly revealed. After speaking personally with the NEDC, we learned that two embryo transfers could be completed for $9,000. That just so happened to be the exact amount which still remained in our adoption savings account. The exact amount to which we had restricted any further adoption considerations. The exact amount we knew would need a miracle.

Embryo adoption truly seemed to be the perfect fit for our family. It was all the ultimate longings of my heart wrapped beautifully together in one unique package. I had learned to love adoption and everything it represented. I had also long desired a pregnancy.

In the deep recesses of my heart, I had long feared the effects that a biological child could have on my boys. (Truthfully, it was one of the first thoughts that went through my mind the moment I learned I was pregnant.) As much as I wanted to prove to the world that adopted and genetic children could be loved and treated equally, I wondered if Griffen and Rhys wanted to participate on that journey. I feared the many ways Satan could use such a situation to lure them away from the truths of God's abundant goodness toward them. And yet, such fears could not be easily reconciled with my desires for pregnancy. Until now.

Now, it seemed like God had reached down from Heaven and created the perfect solution for everyone. A solution so lovingly designed for our family. A solution that blended the glory of adoption with the experience of pregnancy. Humanly speaking, it was perfect!

On March 1, 2013, our application for embryo adoption was completed and received by the National Embryo Donation Center of Knoxville, Tennessee. The next required step was a personal visit to the clinic for a complete medical evaluation and informational meeting. Such appointments were typically scheduled several months out; however, only weeks later, we received the call of a surprise opening available just for us.

We immediately made plans for this fourteen-hour road trip to Tennessee. On Monday, April 15, we met with Dr. Keenan and his staff for a full explanation of the program and underwent a variety of invasive tests. Despite our ten years of marriage and numerous infertility appointments, that day it was discovered that a golf-ball sized fibroid grew on the outside of my uterus. The doctor calmly announced that minor surgery would be required, but assured me that my body should be healed and transfer-ready by the summer.

On April thirtieth, the surgery was successful. The fibroid, along with several small patches of endometriosis, was removed. Just six weeks later, my body was fully healed and ready to begin preparations for an embryo transfer.

As excited as I was about the possibilities that now existed, many fears and discomforts also accompanied this new process. The medical protocol required for an embryo transfer was extensive. The first step included several weeks of injections to the stomach to place my body in a post-menopausal state. Estrogen pills were taken daily to maintain an optimal uterine lining. Once an ultrasound confirmed that these two goals were met, progesterone injections began to prepare the uterus for embryo implantation. A thick, two-inch needle was slowly inserted twice daily into my thighs. The process of icing, injecting, massaging, and heating took about fifteen minutes for each occurrence. The injection sites soon became extremely tender and eventually went totally numb. Numerous ultrasounds and labs were also required throughout the process to monitor progress, and my hormones were on the roller coaster of a lifetime.

As we awaited the day of our transfer, the exciting process of choosing our embryos arrived. Numerous profiles were mailed and included basic genetic information, as well as some social characteristics about each embryo donor (height, weight, hair color, eye color, nationality, personal interests, etc.). Some included family medical history. Some provided the back story of how the embryos came to be donated. Some attached specific requirements for the adoptive family (open adoption, religion, location). Some came with little to no information at all.

This process was so different from anything we had experienced before with traditional adoption. We knew that each tiny life was valuable and would be loved equally in our home. Yet the task remained to simply choose which ones we wanted to adopt. After much thought and prayer, "Donor #1951 (Set of 4 Blastocysts)" officially became ours.

God had truly paved the way for each and every step of this journey. In just four short months, we were approved and transfer-ready—a process that we were told could take up to a year. He worked out every financial detail to the penny when the NEDC graciously offered a special "ministry discount" to us, which reduced our fees by several thousand dollars. He guided us through several home study complications and provided for our child care and travel expenses.

Then on July 16, 2013, our four precious embryos were removed from the freezer and thawed. Two of them did not survive this process. The other two were transferred to my body.

I walked on air as I left the clinic that day. I had long prayed for twins; but in my wildest dreams, I never could have imagined being pregnant with them! I was deeply in love with these two tiny lives, who were now officially mine. In nine days, I would need a blood test to confirm successful implantation and growth; but in the meantime, I reveled in the bliss of this miracle.

Those nine days proved longer than any other in my lifetime. I focused my mind on Scripture and prayed continually. In my personal devotions, I studied the book of Isaiah, and several verses soon became favorites.

"Therefore the Lord waits to be gracious to you, and therefore he exults himself to show mercy to you. For the Lord is a God of justice; blessed are all those who wait for him" (Isa. 30:18).

"From of old no one has heard or perceived by the ear, no eye has seen a God besides you, who acts for those who wait for him" (Isa. 64:4).

On July twenty-fifth, after nine glorious days of living this dream once unimaginable, I recorded these words in my journal:

> After 47 shots, another $4500, and months of pleading for compassion—'Not Pregnant' was the devastating news. Our two year journey through hell has now resulted in the loss of fourteen babies. Crushed! Devastated! Confused! I'm so totally hesitant to even pray because it hasn't yielded any results. If I could ask one thing—please make abundantly clear what we are supposed to do next. I am at a complete loss.

We had never felt so confused in all our life. We were so confident that *this* was God's plan. He had supernaturally directed us to this point. We had given Him everything, but still possessed nothing. We questioned our ability to even discern the will of God for our lives. Maybe God never intended for us to adopt again. Maybe we had missed His will altogether. Maybe the money was meant for something else. Maybe it was just a test of our submission. Maybe we had passed. Maybe we had failed.

If I thought that no one understood me before, now I knew it to be truth. In my entire realm of acquaintances, only one individual I ever encountered had even heard of embryo adoption before. How desperate it must have appeared. How foolish it must have looked to pour so much investment into an experiment. How silly it must have seemed to love so intensely these little lives that could be detected only under a microscope. How pathetic that I thought this ever could have worked. How pitiful that I ever imagined they could really grow and become mine.

As I sat on my bed one afternoon, I wondered again if anyone at all knew my pain. If anyone understood the sorrow I felt over these fourteen babies I had called my own. If anyone knew the despair of a beautiful hope so suddenly destroyed . . . again.

And in those quiet moments, it was almost as if the voice of God Himself descended from on high and whispered audibly in my ear, "Heidi, I know what it's like to lose a Child."

Despite growing up with the Gospel my entire life, its truth suddenly came alive in a new and powerful way. God knew. He knew the grief of watching something beautiful be destroyed (Gen. 6:6). He knew the sorrow of rescue being refused. He knew the sadness of innocence being affected. He knew the pain of unending rejection. He knew the love extended to those who would never be called His own. He knew the cost of redemption. He knew what it was like to lose a Child (Jn. 3:16).

While writing song lyrics often took several weeks for me to finalize, the following words were penned in only a matter of hours. They flowed easily and quickly from my mind. They came from a heart that was strengthened and a soul that was refreshed . . . again.

I KNOW

I will not forget the day we heard the happy news—
One day soon our home would sing with quiet baby coos.
Fulfillment of my heart's desire, answer to my prayers,
Too quickly turned to tragedy. "God, are You really there?"

A dream so roughly snatched away, joy plummeted to pain.

"Did You ever hear me? Were all my pleas in vain?"

Alone. Distressed. I wonder how I'll face another day.

But in that quiet moment, I hear a kind Voice say—

"I know what it's like to lose a Child;
I know all the pain of a paradise defiled.
I know sad goodbyes cause the teardrops to flow wild.
I know. I know."

I pick my weary body up and slowly start to rise.

I toss the empty tissue box and dry my aching eyes.

In a world that keeps on spinning, I feel totally alone

Until His grace reminds me that my pain is not unknown.

"I know what it's like to lose a Child;
I know all the pain of a paradise defiled.
I know sad goodbyes cause the teardrops to flow wild.
I know. I know."

"I know good will come from this agonizing trial.
I know though you weep, there will be another smile.
I know, yes, I know, it will one day be worthwhile.
I know. I know."[33]

Almost two long years ago, we had devoted ourselves to this journey. We turned $20,000 over to God and committed its entirety to His use. We determined to remain steadfast to the process for two years—until the expiration of our adoption home study. With much reluctance, the only reason we decided to return to Tennessee for one more embryo transfer was because $4,500 still remained in our adoption savings account and two months still remained on our home study. We concluded that God's prompting in our lives never intended another child, but rather the complete emptying of ourselves. We knew that a clear conscience required the total surrender of it all.

> Lord, I acknowledge that Your ways are better! Do what You want with my life! As we prepare to go back for transfer #2 in September, I am not even praying for results. It is simply my act of submission to You. We give it ALL back—now do what You want (Journal entry, August 8).

With injection sites still sore from round one, we began the entire medical protocol all over again in August. Lupron. Estrace. Progesterone. Ultrasounds. Labs.

Another stack of donor profiles was delivered, which contained several hundred embryos from which to choose. And once again, we needed to pick which ones we wanted. Curly hair or straight? Love for sports or love for music? East Coast or West? Blue eyes or brown?

Rob and I sat at the kitchen counter and poured over the details of each option. After many minutes, we finally narrowed the pool to about six different profiles. Faced with a nearly impossible decision, I eventually looked at Rob and simply said, "You choose." He glanced over the information one final time, then pointed and said, "Those ones will probably be tall. That could be cool. Let's choose them." And with that, "Donor #2186 (Set of 8 Blastocysts)" officially became ours.

These genetic siblings came from a middle-aged couple in Kansas. In their own attempts at growing a family, they underwent in vitro fertilization. The sperm was taken directly from the husband—a thirty-seven-year-old information technology supervisor, measuring six feet, three inches, with brown hair and blue eyes. Presumably, the wife's eggs were damaged because the couple sought success using donor eggs. The oocyte (egg) donor was a twenty-four-year-old interior design student, who sold her eggs to provide additional income for college. She was described as five feet, nine inches, with green eyes and strawberry blonde hair. It could be assumed that the husband and wife eventually achieved success of their own, but eight embryos still remained. Without the desire to use them personally, they were donated to the NEDC without any stipulations or desires for further contact from the adoptive family.

Once again, travel plans were made. We decided to take our boys with us on this trip and spend a little extra time sightseeing as a family. Due to the twenty-eight hours of required driving, we planned to stop midway in St. Louis, where we booked one night at the Union Station Hotel—an old, renovated train station that had been turned into a shopping center and hotel. A day at the Arch, swimming time, and Chuck E. Cheese also made it on to the itinerary. No matter what, we were determined to make the best of this trip and enjoy being together.

As we neared the day of our departure, my heart was truly at rest—no longer due to hopes for my future, but because of gratitude for my present. Just a few more weeks and this journey was over. I finally saw the light at the end of the tunnel. I was more than ready to put this chapter of my life behind me and to learn to live again with the many blessings already bestowed.

> As I look at my two precious little boys, I'm amazed at how good You have already been to me!!! Their looks and talents fit perfectly into our family! We have a beautiful home and very few financial pressures. You have given me a husband that I love 1000 times more today than when we were married. And our church is beyond comparison. From a truly contented heart—thank You (September 3, 2013).

> God, You are so very good to me! As we left church this morning, ready to head to TN to get our babies, we were given two cards and a batch of cookies. The first contained $100 to help with our trip expenses and the other contained a $1000 gift card. It's as if You're saying, "Stay the course. This is exactly where you are supposed to be." From the bottom of my heart, thank You for the blessings of

today. May they spur me to trust You even more with my tomorrows—whatever they may hold (September 22, 2013).

We arrived at the NEDC for our final embryo transfer on September 24, 2013. Having Griffen and Rhys along this time, Rob planned to remain with them in the waiting area of the clinic while I went back for the procedure alone. There in that small room, we prayed together as a family before my name was finally called.

My heart was anxious and afraid. While the actual transfer lasted only about fifteen minutes, it was definitely uncomfortable and scary. It required a completely full bladder, and the many tools and pressures that accompanied it were most unpleasant. When the nurse arrived to escort me away, I said goodbye to my family and warily followed her down the hall.

Such pressures were clearly unfelt by my husband. Rob often resembled the epitome of stress-free living. He simply called out in his naturally relaxed tone, "Say hi to the kids for me."

Earlier that morning, four of our tiny embryos were removed from the freezer and thawed. Once again, two of them had not survived this process. The other two, however, received almost perfect ratings from the embryologist (5AA and 5AB) and were smoothly transferred to my body.

And with that, we again entered the nine-day waiting period before the outcome could be verified by a blood test. Truthfully, this period of waiting was not as difficult this time around. Whether or not another child entered our home, this long journey was finally over! And that fact alone brought tremendous encouragement.

The very week we returned from Tennessee was our church's annual missions conference. Dr. Les Lofquist was the keynote speaker, and the week was filled with special dinners, luncheons, and nightly meetings. On Wednesday evening, October second, we sat together in the sanctuary for the final session of the conference.

That night, Dr. Lofquist delivered a message on stewardship from First Corinthians four. What poor stewards we must have looked like to the outside world! We had seemingly wasted $20,000 and unfathomable amounts of emotional energy for nothing. But as the words of Scripture were read, my heart soared, and my tears could not be controlled.

"Moreover, it is required of stewards that they be found faithful" (1 Cor. 4:2).

Dr. Lofquist expounded with words forever etched on my mind and highlighted in my Bible: "Faithfulness will be the standard for accounting in stewards—not increase." In that moment, I realized anew that I was not judged on the results I produced. I was judged on my faithfulness! And I was confident that I had followed God's leading to the very end. What a fitting conclusion to our adoption journey.

The very next day, October third, was our first blood test.

In my heart of hearts, I was totally prepared to receive the news that, once again, the test was negative. No feelings of pregnancy existed, and I was highly used to disappointment by now. I drove to the lab in Wichita first thing that Thursday morning. I then proceeded to do my grocery shopping and run other errands. I basically tried to keep my mind occupied with other things and not consumed with anxiety over the anticipated news.

Then late that afternoon, after all my tasks were completed, Nurse Katie from the NEDC finally called.

"Hi, Heidi. Is Rob there with you?" she asked in a calm tone of voice.

I signaled for him to join me in the bedroom, then closed the door behind. I put the call on speaker and listened intently. The end of our story was about to be written.

"I have a question for you guys," Katie continued. "Can your house fit two more?"

I was completely in shock! Being so used to failure, I had prepared myself for one final round of disappointment. But instead, Katie now delivered some of the happiest news I had ever received in my lifetime. My labs revealed that I was pregnant with twins!

She continued to explain that by nine days after an embryo transfer, she hoped to see an HCG level of 100. This most often indicated a healthy pregnancy at this stage. But my levels measured an astounding 452—a strong sign that both babies had implanted successfully.

She further instructed me to return to the lab again four days later to monitor proper increase. The goal was to see a new HCG level of around 1,500. Such results nearly guaranteed that both babies thrived inside of me.

As we ended the phone call, Rob and I fell into each other's arms in a mixture of disbelief and elation. We knelt by our bed and prayed once more. But for the first time in two years, this was a prayer of abundant thanksgiving and joy.

Four days later, on October seventh, I returned to the lab for beta test number two. That afternoon, Nurse Katie called again with the results. This time, my HCG levels measured 2,864—a number that far exceeded the desired goal of 1,500. The smile on my face could not be erased.

My pregnancy was monitored faithfully. Estrogen supplements and progesterone injections continued twice daily. Our prayers for these two precious, little lives remained fervent.

We eagerly awaited our six-week ultrasound. By that stage, heartbeats could be detected, and proper growth could be measured. The appointment was scheduled with our local monitoring clinic, and we eagerly anticipated this major milestone.

On October 18, 2013, our family drove to this meeting all together. While Griffen and Rhys sat in the hallway and played a video game, I sat trembling on the exam table. I so desperately wanted to hear two healthy heartbeats. To see two squirming babies. To finally experience a lifelong dream become a reality.

The words of Colossians 1:16-18 flooded my mind. I repeated them over and over again as I awaited the doctor's entrance.

"For by him all things were created, in heaven and on earth, visible and invisible . . . All things were created through him and for him. And he is before all things, and in him all things hold together . . . **That in everything he might be preeminent**" (emphasis mine).

The doctor finally arrived. Rob and I clutched hands and waited. Our eyes were glued to the computer monitor, despite little idea of what in the world we were actually looking at. We held our breaths and awaited its interpretation.

After mere moments, the doctor calmly asked, "How many embryos were transferred?"

"Two," we answered in unison.

"Well, I am looking at *three* perfectly beating hearts here," he continued. "One of them must have split."

In an instant, pure and complete elation overcame me. While the doctor saw a rare, but natural, occurrence, I saw a miracle. As I watched each baby being measured, I watched my countless prayers being answered. As I listened to three separate heartbeats, I listened to God's tender compassion. I saw so much more than triplets. I saw God!

"Now to him who is able to do far more abundantly than all that we ask or think, according to the power at work within us, to him be glory in the church and in Christ Jesus throughout all generations, forever and ever. Amen" (Eph. 3:20-21).

* * *

Pause and meditate on the fact that God has authority over all of creation. We remember the flannel graph images from our childhood that picture this Deity Who created the world "in the beginning" (Gen. 1:1). We remember the Voice that spoke the light into existence and uttered every flower into being. We remember the power that formed the firmament and the imagination that designed every creeping thing. We remember the Breath Who gave life to Adam and the Surgeon Who skillfully turned a single rib into Eve.

We may even remember God's creation of the immaterial universe. The invisible elements. The laws of nature. The angels. The hierarchy of power within the spirit world.

We remember the moments of long ago. The moment when the great waters of the Red Sea parted at their Maker's command (Ex. 14). The moment when the rocks produced water and the bread rained down from heaven (Ex. 16-17). The moment when the sun stood still in its orbit as its Creator supernaturally kept the universe from spinning out of control (Josh. 10). The moment when ferocious lions became docile (Dan. 6) and a large fish moved in obedience to His direction (Jonah 2).

But so often, our faith ends here. We forget that the waters which flow today still submit to their Creator. Every raindrop, every flood, every tsunami moves only when given permission from on High. "When he utters his voice, there is a tumult of waters in the heavens, and he makes the mist rise from the ends of the earth. He makes lightning for the rain, and he brings forth the wind from his storehouses" (Jer. 10:13).

Each morning, the sun still rises at His command (Matt. 5:45). He still " . . . makes the morning darkness, and treads on the heights of the earth . . . " (Amos 4:13). He still " . . . changes times and seasons" (Dan. 2:21).

He still appoints kings (Psa. 22:28) and turns their heart at His desire (Prov. 21:1). He still creates both success and calamity (Is. 45:7). He still possesses all riches and honor and power and strength (1 Chron. 29:12).

The book of Colossians focuses much attention on the supremacy of Jesus Christ. God's Son was the cause of all creation and continues to be the reason it remains (Col. 1:16). He is the Active Leader of the universal body of believers. He is the Risen Lord and Head of a new immortal order. He is Alive. He is Engaged. He is Busy. He is Zealous. He is Preeminent!

He " . . . **is** before all things, and in him all things hold together" (Col. 1:17—emphasis mine). "And he **is** the head of the body, the church. He **is** the beginning, the firstborn from the dead . . . " (Col. 1:18—emphasis mine).

He still " . . . upholds the universe by the word of his power . . . " (Heb. 1:3). He still guides the sparrows (Matt. 10:29). He still cares for anxieties (1 Pet. 5:7). He still intercedes for believers (Rom. 8:34). He still strengthens the weak (Phil. 4:13). He still gives peace (Jn. 14:27).

He still looks down in pity on the pain of a barren woman and notices her every tear. He still cares about her every broken dream and her every unfulfilled desire. He still listens to her every prayer and still longs to do her good.

And sometimes, He still makes the miraculous. Sometimes, He blesses her far beyond anything she could have ever imagined (Eph. 3:20). Sometimes, He remembers the submission of her hurting heart and the release of her personal pursuits to humbly follow the path of His choosing. Sometimes, He uses the broken pieces of her life to guide her to something better. Sometimes, He puts just the right people in just the right places at just the right time to open her mind to something bigger than herself. Sometimes, He prepares her body for "such a time as this" (Est. 4:14). Sometimes, He opens her womb at the very preordained moment in history to receive the very preordained embryos He longs to awaken. Sometimes, He not only grants her request for multiples, but also allows her to carry them within her own body. Sometimes, He reminds her of His magnificence. Sometimes, He increases her impression of the impossible. Sometimes, He exceeds her every expectation.

Dear friend, He is still on the throne! "Jesus Christ is the same yesterday and today and forever" (Heb. 13:8). He still possesses limitless power. He still commands all creation. He still retains every resource. He still orchestrates every occasion. He still invents the impossible. He still structures the supernatural. He still exceeds expectations. He still makes the miraculous!

CHAPTER ELEVEN

SOMETIMES GOD MAKES THE MIRACULOUS: UNDERSTANDING OUR RESPONSE

And when they had [let down their nets], they enclosed a large number of fish,
and their nets were breaking . . . But when Simon Peter saw it, he fell down at
Jesus' knees, saying, "Depart from me, for I am a sinful man, O Lord." For he
and all who were with him were astonished at the catch of fish that they had
taken . . . and so also were James and John, sons of Zebedee, who were part-
ners with Simon . . . And when they had brought their boats to land, they left
everything and followed him (Lk. 5:6, 8-11).

THE DAY THAT I LAID on that exam table and learned that I was pregnant with triplets was, without question, one of the happiest days of my entire life! Despite the doctor's explanation that this was categorized a high-risk pregnancy, I had very few anxieties or concerns. Knowing firsthand the work that accompanied one baby, I excitedly embraced the new challenge of three. Being fully aware that our family budget was instantly turned upside down, nothing but love followed each sacrifice. There existed no doubt in my mind that this was the supernatural work of a loving, compassionate God Who had heard and answered my prayers.

My excitement could not be contained as I made several phone calls on the drive home. Nothing in the world dampened my joy. Not the panicked reaction of my mother—*"Oh, Heidi, you're going to be as big as a whale!"* Not the hesitant reaction of my sister—*"Are you sure you're excited about this?"* Not the shock and total confusion that accompanied most everyone else as I proudly announced that I was pregnant with triplets . . . who were adopted!

The doctors advised us to wait until our nine-week ultrasound before making our news public. At that point, proper growth and development could be confirmed. And so, we shared our secret with only the small handful of family and friends who even knew we walked this road in the first place.

Knowing that the floodgates of questions would soon be opened, we used the next three weeks to create an online blog.[34] We journaled our family story from the very beginning—God's call toward adoption, the miraculous gifts of Griffen and Rhys, the provision of funds and direction toward a third attempt, the many losses and heartaches, and the discovery of embryo adoption.

Many people in our lives knew little about our two-year journey through darkness. But now, we longed to be transparent. We wanted others to understand the suffering we had endured and the glorious end which had resulted. We desired to highlight God's direction and His ultimate goodness and faithfulness each step of the way.

We also understood that many questions would be asked about embryo adoption, and so we hoped to give a clear and concise explanation in one location, as opposed to regular repetition over and over again. In this arena of new fertility assistance and unconventional adoption, we knew that the supernatural hand of God could be easily overshadowed by these intriguing developments. So, we went beyond the scientific explanation and made extra effort to highlight our sovereign God. A God of love Who valued every life. A God of compassion Who blessed us beyond our imagination. A God of power Who defied every human odd. (According to NEDC statistics, our probability for twins was about only twelve percent, and our likelihood for triplets was a mere one-and-a-half percent chance.)

We proudly awaited the opportunity to announce the newest members of our family. A photo shoot revealed our little trio using three white baby onesies hung on a clothesline amid the changing fall colors. And ultrasound pictures accompanied the anticipated introduction of Babies A, B, and C.

On November 7, 2013, we arrived at our nine-week appointment. Once again, we heard three perfect heartbeats and watched three healthy and squirming babies on the monitor. Each one was measured and observed. Following a flawless review, we went live with our new blog.

Truthfully, I possessed doubts that anyone would actually read it. The initial post was extremely long and detailed. Plus, I feared that even those who did read its entirety might conclude that we were totally nuts.

But God's miraculous goodness continued.

Love and support for our family overflowed. Over thirty-three hundred people eventually read that initial blog post. Copies were even printed and distributed. A church baby shower was planned. Boxes of maternity clothes were dropped off. Frozen meals filled our freezer. Financial gifts arrived, which completely funded our new nursery, car seats, and triplet stroller. We even received a donation of $4,000 to help with the purchase of a new vehicle. Offers of help poured in. Notes of encouragement flooded. Faithful prayers continued. Despite any prior moments of worry, we received only abundant support.

One special card that I received included these powerful sentiments:

> Every time infertility is mentioned in Scripture, God is about to work a miracle. It might not make sense when something that comes so easily to others is made so difficult for you, but maybe it is because you have been chosen for the supernatural! Blessed are you, not cursed, when God invites the supernatural! This is something that many will never experience.

Because this was a triplet pregnancy, we were immediately transferred to a high-risk OB doctor to be monitored regularly. On December twenty-third, fifteen weeks into the pregnancy, we went in for our fourth ultrasound. That day, we received an early Christmas gift when we excitedly learned the genders of our babies. Within seconds, the nurse announced that Baby A was a

GIRL. She was the fraternal triplet, who sat at the bottom of the pile. Instant relief and excitement flooded the room. We had a daughter!

I had long prayed for multiple girls; and in my heart of hearts, I desired this pregnancy to reveal two girls and a boy. In my highly practical mind, that combination fit best into our family and into the layout of our home. The other three men in my life all wanted triplet girls. But with all this dreaming, I feared that anything else posed the possibility of a letdown.

One of my most treasured memories, however, was the moment the nurse declared that Babies B and Baby C were identical twin boys. The sincerest gasp of excitement escaped Rob's mouth, and I knew instantly that he was not disappointed. Two more little men were suddenly added to his growing basketball team. And his long-awaited princess now held an extra special place of honor.

The next day, we loaded our van and headed to Minnesota to celebrate Christmas. The big gender reveal proved an extra special addition to each family gathering. Three helium balloons were enclosed in a large package and adorned with a fancy decorative bow. As the box was opened, our announcements floated upward. "It's a BOY." It's a BOY." "It's a GIRL." Our families were genuinely surprised as they expected that such news could not be learned until several weeks later. (Though I eventually discovered that a certain grandmother accidentally opened the package prior to our reveal and faked her reaction altogether!)

With the new year upon us, we kicked our baby preparations into full gear. By mid-February, the owl-themed nursery was completed, featuring an adorable palette of blue, green, and orange decor. The church baby shower filled our home with all manner of matching clothes and coordinating gear. Diapers, wipes, blankets, and bibs were everywhere!

While I savored each moment of this long-awaited dream, the demands on my body were extreme. By the twenty-four-week benchmark, I already measured the size of a full-term pregnancy. I became exhausted just walking across a room. Climbing a flight of stairs left me breathless. Standing for any period of time brought dizziness.

On February 24, 2014, I was admitted to the hospital and placed on complete bedrest. My labs revealed an increased level of protein in my urine and a diagnosis of preeclampsia was confirmed. This was not entirely unexpected as the doctors had warned me of the many complications that were likely to arise. In the hospital, I was now restricted to walking only to the bathroom and moving around my small room.

But God's goodness continued to abound.

With the sudden removal of the chief child care administrator, home-schooler, cook, launderer, maid, and organizer, our family now possessed a new array of needs. An online calendar was created; and in no time at all, an army of volunteers from our church filled each and every spot. Daily child care was provided for Griffen and Rhys, and their school studies were faithfully maintained. Weekly laundry service was arranged, and meals were delivered often. One mother and daughter duo volunteered to clean our house for an entire year, and still another dear friend shopped for and purchased entire spring wardrobes for our ever-growing boys.

I was also immensely cared for throughout my two-month-long hospital stay. A group of girlfriends planned weekly game days in the lobby. Puzzles, books, crafts, and snacks were delivered regularly. One friend came and decorated my room. Another came and taught me how to make hair bows for my new baby girl. Still another taught me how to crochet. (You should have seen the lovely triangle-shaped washcloth I created.) I received more than one hundred hospital visits, not including the regular appearances from Rob and my boys.

Despite the inconvenient drive to the hospital, Rob came almost every day to see me. He often took me for walks in a wheelchair; and when the weather was nice, we even ventured outside into the fresh air. Since I had an extra bed in my room, he was occasionally able to spend the night. And on two occasions, extra air mattresses were brought in, which allowed Griffen and Rhys to also join the fun. Family movie nights, ice cream in the cafeteria, and wheelchair rides around the hospital provided many fun memories for us all.

My health was monitored religiously, and my vital signs were taken every four to six hours. On top of the preeclampsia, I was also diagnosed with gestational diabetes. My diet was soon restricted, and the blood tests were administered around the clock. My "happy stash" of sugar was sadly removed from my room and suddenly replaced with additional protein. Even with the required healthy diet, I gained seventy pounds throughout the pregnancy.

My babies were also faithfully monitored. I loved being able to listen to their heartbeats multiple times each day. I became so accustomed to the procedure that soon I guided the nurse's wand across my ever-expanding belly and led them to the correct location of each baby.

The regular sonograms also proved to be a highlight. I was blessed with a grand total of twenty-five of them throughout the pregnancy! (Yes, I counted and have the pictures to prove it.) What a treat it was to escape the confines of my private room and be wheeled down to the radiology floor to watch my babies wiggle around inside of me.

The hospital staff was amazing, and I soon became well-acquainted with many of them. There were numerous times that a friendly nurse just lingered in my room for another casual conversation. The staff chaplain also made regular visits. I soon knew most of them by name and appreciated the extra measures they took to make me feel so comfortable.

The medical team faithfully prepared me for each new step. I received many educational visits from the staff and was clearly informed of the chaos to be expected upon delivery. One day, they even wheeled me down to the NICU and explained each machine that could be required. They showed me babies born at each gestation and made me fully aware of their needs. Since the triplets were likely to be born early, they explained that their underdeveloped lungs would likely be silent upon delivery. That each one would likely be taken away immediately by a team of doctors and attended to separately. That they would likely be required to stay in the hospital until their original due date in mid-June.

My pregnancy was considered full term at thirty-six weeks; however, the average triplets arrived between thirty-two to thirty-four weeks. My C-section was scheduled for Thursday, May first, at five o'clock p.m. (thirty-four weeks). But as complications continued to arise, this date was soon altered.

On Friday, April 11, my labs revealed additional concerns. The preeclampsia had progressed to a severe state, and my liver had ceased to function properly. The doctor immediately re-scheduled my C-section for first thing Monday morning (April fourteenth). This provided just enough time for one final round of steroids to help the babies' lung developments. (Plus, I begged them to wait until Monday, since my husband was a music pastor, and this Palm Sunday weekend was packed with additional responsibilities.)

I was escorted down to the labor and delivery floor, where I was now monitored around the clock—literally, around the clock. The wires were everywhere, and the beeping sounds were unending. Each baby's vitals were displayed on screens above my head, and the alarm sounded every time one of them wiggled out of range. Since this happened every ten minutes, eventually the nurses rotated the duty of sitting by my side and holding each monitor in place on my belly. Exhausted, at one point I asked if the monitors could just be removed long enough for me to get a couple hours of sleep—a request they graciously granted.

A catheter was inserted, removing any need whatsoever to get out of bed. An IV was started, and magnesium sulfate was added to prevent seizures. The final round of steroids was administered. And now we just waited.

But by late Saturday evening, I started to have trouble breathing. An oxygen mask was provided, but little relief followed. Before long, I labored for every mucus-filled breath of air. The doctor was called, and both a chest x-ray and EKG were ordered immediately. In the early Sunday morning hours, I was wheeled through the dark, silent hallways to the radiology department one final time.

At approximately eight a.m., the results arrived and revealed fluid in my lungs. Within minutes, the delivery doctor was on her way, and the nurses began preparations for an emergency C-section. They informed me that my babies would be delivered within the hour and that if my husband wanted to be present, he needed to come immediately.

Rob was already at the church with Griffen and Rhys preparing for the many moving parts of the morning worship service. As he answered his phone, I blurted, "I'm so sorry. I tried to wait, but the babies are coming right now." Without a moment of hesitation, he jumped in the car and raced to the hospital in his three-piece suit and tie. Substitutes immediately filled in for all the responsibilities he so abruptly left behind.

On Palm Sunday morning, April 13, 2014, a choir of family and friends shouted, "Hosanna," as we welcomed our precious trio into the world. At 8:52, 8:53, and 8:54 a.m., Keira Ashleigh (four pounds, five ounces), Taerik Andrew (four pounds, five ounces), and Drake Alexander (three pounds, eleven ounces) were born at 31.5 weeks gestation. The delivery room was filled with a grand total of twenty-seven people, all working together in unison. But it was the Unseen Guest Who sovereignly orchestrated the outcome. "Hosanna in the highest!"

Despite all previous warnings, each baby entered the world with a loud cry and was briefly introduced to me before being taken away. The only breathing assistance that any of them needed was a CPAP machine to help keep their airways open. At only two days old, even that was removed from Taerik and Keira. After only four short days in the NICU, all three breathed independently and were promoted to the special care nursery at the hospital. There, a private room allowed them to all be together and provided ample room for us to visit.

The miraculous milestones only continued. Within that first week of life, all three babies were feeding from a bottle. Nurses were astounded, as this was generally not even considered an option until the thirty-fourth gestational week. But each one exhibited signs of readiness and achieved success well ahead of the anticipated schedule.

While the babies still needed to be monitored for a little while longer, I was finally released. I had laid in that hospital bed for fifty-one days and was very eager to return home. Griffen and Rhys were so excited when they returned from church one Wednesday night to find me back in my own bedroom. Rhys immediately blurted out, "Can I see where they cut you open?" After showing my brave boy a portion of the scar, he breathed a sigh of relief and replied, "I'm sure glad they didn't cut you all the way in half, Mom!" Yeah, me, too!

Throughout the next several weeks, I slowly recovered and regained my strength. Trips were made almost every day to the hospital to visit the babies. And final preparations were made at home for their arrival.

At only seventeen days old, Taerik and Keira were discharged without any monitors or medications. Despite being only thirty-three weeks and six days gestational age, their five-pound little bodies were each awarded a perfectly clean bill of health! On Wednesday afternoon, April thirtieth, we walked out of the hospital and into our gleefully anticipated chaos. (Within moments of entering our house, Rhys picked up his baby sister by the feet, and we knew that life would never be the same again.)

Out of town relatives soon poured in to help us celebrate. Both sets of parents, plus my sister and her kids, all arrived on the scene. Rob's mom even took off of work for a month to remain and help us out with this major life adjustment.

Then on Saturday, May tenth, little Drake joined the happy trio. His gestational age was only thirty-five weeks and two days old. A few minor concerns required him to come home with a heart monitor, but the only panic-filled moments in which the alarm sounded were eventually attributed to operator error.

Between my ordered bedrest and the triplets' care after birth, Wesley Hospital in Wichita, Kansas, had been our family's home for a grand total of seventy-five days! While deep fears and lifelong trauma have accompanied many others in similar situations, our days there were filled with nothing but abundant joy and confidence. It was during those seventy-five days that we watched our mighty God make the miraculous.

The very next day after Drake arrived home was Mother's Day. With the whole family coordinated in a lovely blue and yellow palette, we ventured out to the place we most desired to be—with our church. On Sunday, May 11, 2014, we proudly carried our three newborns up on the stage for a special baby dedication.

These miraculous gifts were a visual representation of exceeding abundance above anything we could have imagined. They were desires fulfilled. They were displays of God's power. They were reminders of His compassion. They were answers to prayer.

"He gives the barren woman a home, making her the joyous mother of children.
Praise the LORD" (Psa. 113:9).

* * *

Sometimes when you pray, God makes the miraculous! The Hero of the Holy Scriptures is still alive and active today. His voice still controls the universe. His eyes still pierce the darkness. His arm still has power to save. He can still part the waters, send manna from heaven, bring water from the rock, make the city walls crumble, instruct the sun to stand still, withhold the rain, multiply the remaining oil, deliver from fire, tame the lions, and he can still send whales to rescue. He can still turn water into wine, drive out the demons, bring sight to the blind, heal the paralytic, open deaf ears, raise the dead, feed the masses, calm the storm, and walk on water. He can appear when you least expect it and accomplish what you could never imagine.

"With God all things are possible" (Matt. 19:26b).

The purpose of answered prayer is always to bring God glory. Such glory is never lacking or dependent upon a response, but rather it is overflowing from a completely satisfied Being. God delights to extend His glory beyond Himself and display the beauty of His perfection through man.

God's perfection is displayed in each and every answer to prayer. In granting peace. In teaching patience. In seeking submission. In growing faith. In being enough. In expanding endurance. In saying no. In making miracles.

God's glory demands an appropriate response. Gratitude is an essential component to glorifying God (Psa. 50:23; Rom. 1:21). A heart full of thanksgiving in any situation bears witness to the Giver of all that is ultimately good. Gratitude comes naturally to one receiving a miracle. But the Bible also outlines several other appropriate responses to the recipient of such abundance.

> *"On one occasion, while the crowd was pressing in on [Jesus] to hear the word of God, he was standing by the lake of Gennesaret, and he saw two boats by the lake, but the fishermen had gone out of them and were washing their nets. Getting into one of the boats, which was Simon's, he asked him to put out a little from the land. And he sat down and taught the people from the boat. And when he had finished speaking, he said to Simon, 'Put out into the deep and let down your nets for a catch.' And Simon answered, 'Master, we toiled all night and took nothing! But at your word I will let down the nets.' And when they had done this, they enclosed a large number of fish, and their nets were breaking. They signaled to their partners in the other boat to come and help them. And they came and filled both the boats, so that they began to sink. But when Simon Peter saw it, he fell down at Jesus' knees, saying, 'Depart from me, for I am a sinful man, O Lord.' For he and all who were with him were astonished at the catch of fish that they had taken, and so also were James and John, sons of Zebedee, who were partners with Simon. And Jesus said to Simon, 'Do not be afraid; from now on you will be catching men.'*

And when they had brought their boats to land, they left everything and followed him" (Lk. 5:1-11).

The first response that overflowed from these men was *astonishment*. As experienced fishermen, they knew that, at this time of day, the fish swam in much deeper waters. But in obedience to Jesus' command, they lowered their nets anyway. Then they watched in amazement and wonder as swarms of sea creatures moved in obedience to the voice of Jesus Himself. The catch was so abundant that their nets started to break and their boats began to sink. They witnessed the miraculous and stood in awe of such power and authority.

In great contrast, however, the second reaction was a *deep understanding of unworthiness*. Simon Peter immediately recognized the guilty stains of his own sin. He understood his inherent wickedness, his slavery, and his guilt. And he fell humbly to his knees in the presence of Perfection. He knew that such grace was totally undeserved.

But the final reaction stands out the most to me. *"They left everything and followed Him"* (verse eleven). This miracle was an immediate windfall to the family business. It undoubtedly provided financial security and recognition. They received, in an instant, a catch that generally required much labor and skill. But as they looked at the swarms of fish that overflowed from their sinking boats, the measure of ease and happiness it offered suddenly paled in comparison to walking beside the Miracle Man. Being in His presence proved far more glorious than any earthly gifts He bestowed. The miracle they received prompted them to walk away from everything. They refused their temporal increase, leaving it right there on the seashore. From that moment forward, they became full-time followers of Jesus Christ.

This life-changing decision brought rewards far greater than any temporal abundance! In the days that followed, they listened as Jesus commanded the storms on those same waters to cease. They watched Him walk on the seas that had once employed them. And they witnessed Him feed the masses with just two insignificant fish!

Sometimes, God meets you with the miraculous. He blesses you in ways unimaginable. He showers you with abundance. He demonstrates His mighty power and compassion. He bestows great mercy and grace.

And in response, He deserves your worship. He deserves a heart overflowing with thanksgiving. He deserves an acknowledgment of His worth. He deserves an awe and amazement of His power. He deserves a recognition of personal unworthiness. He deserves eyes on the eternal. He deserves hands holding loosely to the temporal. He deserves your service. He deserves your future. He deserves your all.

You see, it's all about Him! The end goal is never merely the fulfillment of my earthly desires. The objective is not simply my ease and happiness. Every dream I could ever imagine falls immeasurably short of the miracles God longs to display. Every answered prayer is but a glimpse of His glory. Every gift that I lay back at His feet holds the hope of greater reward.

CHAPTER TWELVE

SOMETIMES GOD PROMOTES BETTER PRAYER

"Lord, teach us to pray . . . " (Lk. 11:1b).

OH, THE LESSONS I HAVE learned along this path to answered prayer! What glimpses I have gleaned of a God Who gently listens! And what clarity has followed the realization that He uses my desperate pleas to accomplish much greater goals! I have learned that God will do anything to capture my heart. Anything to transform my life into the image of His Son. *Anything* to accomplish His ultimate goal.

> *"And we know that for those who love God all things work together for good,*
> *for those who are called according to his purpose. For those whom he fore-*
> *knew he also predestined* ***to be conformed to the image of his Son . . . "***
> (Rom. 8:28-29—emphasis mine).

In His infinite wisdom, God knew that using children to conform my heart would be the most effective means. Love and tenderness toward kids were innately present from my earliest days. Kindergarten graduations and elementary award ceremonies always made me cry, as I watched young faces that beamed with pride and proud parents who cheered each milestone. Stories of neglect or harm always affected me deeply, as I vividly imagined the innocent being robbed of their security and nurture. On one occasion, I sought assurance from my mom that our doors would always be opened to any such child if the opportunity for rescue ever arose. And knowing everything about me, God handpicked the tests that shook me the most. Tests that tugged at my deepest emotions. Tests that threatened my greatest dreams. Tests that drove me to my knees.

I vividly remember my simple prayer of so many years ago: "Dear God, please let this be the month that I get pregnant." I recall the hours spent begging Him for relief and pleading for His blessing. I relive the unending disappointments and the paralyzing loss. And I wonder—did God really answer my prayers?

He never allowed a successful natural conception. He withheld a genetic heir who resembled our physical features. He failed to operate on my timetable.

But as I consider more deeply those desires of long ago, I realize their eternal insignificance. I notice my selfishness and pride. I recognize that my endless cries for a pregnancy just pale in comparison with God's plan for my life. And I thank Him for exchanging my shortsighted requests with His desires for *so much more.*

Along this particular path to answered prayer—a path that spanned over ten years—I discovered an Ear Which is always listening and a Friend Who is always available. I met the Prince of Peace, Who offers incomprehensible calm in the midst of earth's darkest hour. I learned about a mighty King Who pays attention to the angry outbursts of His creation and receives sinners with patient regard. I heard the compassionate whisper of One Who intimately knows my earthly struggles and feels my deepest pain.

I learned rich truths about my salvation! Its incredible cost. Its desperate need. Its life-changing power. Its extension to the helpless. Its offer to the enemy.

I learned more deeply of its glorious provisions to the recipient! Adoption. Rescue. Opportunity. Equality. Unfettered access. Unending security. Unfathomable inheritance. A new Father. A new family. A new future.

God taught me life lessons that touch every corner of my life going forward. That waiting is good for me. That in the silent wilderness wanderings, He is still working. That submission is required. That there are no boundaries to His abilities. That in loneliness, He is enough. That sanctification requires stretching. That endurance demands expanding. That sometimes, no is truly best. That sometimes worship *in* my weakness brings Him the greatest joy. That miracles still happen. That exceeding abundance beyond every imagination is, indeed, possible.

And when I think that God used me as part of His eternal plan to offer salvation to another human soul, my heart could almost burst. Abundant joy comes in knowing that He picked me for the supernatural! Deep fulfillment and satisfaction follow the realization that the path of His choosing bore eternal significance. Gratitude and humility accompany the awareness that in love, God withheld my simple desires to bestow so much greater wealth.

And even beyond the ultimate goal of my personal sanctification, God brought so much joy to my earthly life. He reminded me that His ways are so much higher than anything I think I desire. He filled my arms to overflowing with the babies that I had long desired. He allowed the pregnancy for which I had long prayed. He left tangible tokens of His tenderness in my living room and reminders of His redemption down every hall. And while these five priceless gifts of His grace may not bear genetic similarities to me, they have the fingerprints of God all over them.

SO MUCH MORE

By Heidi Fuller

Never lessen your life to your limited sight
When My plans have greatness in store.
And do not be distracted by temporal joys,
But open your eyes to more.

Keep your feet straight and narrow;
Keep your heart close to Me. Bend your desire and will.
Emptied of self, bow at My throne,
Longing My Spirit to fill.

Widen your vision; expand your effect;
Grow and broaden your view.
Give your one simple life. Give it over to Me.
I'll showcase My glory through you.

To the mouth opened wide, I will fill and provide,
I alone satisfy and outpour.
Finest wheat I supply to the hands lifted high
To the soul's fervent cry seeking more.[35]

My sanctification journey upon this earth certainly did not end here. It continues until the glorious day that I stand face-to-face before my Savior. The day that I gain complete revelation of all that He is. The day of my ultimate transformation into sinless perfection.

Until that day, God continues to transform me into His image from one degree of glory to another (2 Cor. 3:18). He continues to refine and mold me. He continues to bring new tests that teach me even more about the depths of His character and the rich traits He longs to develop in me upon this earth.

When our trio was just one year old, God impressed upon our hearts the need to go back to the NEDC for our four remaining adopted embryos. Just when we thought our journey was ended and our arms overflowed, we were confronted with the fate of the triplets' genetic siblings, who still remained frozen in storage. Siblings who belonged to us and awaited our decision regarding their future. We had never imagined being placed in this position—a position of too many kids. But right in the middle of life's busiest days—days of constant running just to keep up with our daily demands—God challenged us to pursue the four we had left behind. Amid sleep-deprived bodies, overly extended finances, and fear-filled minds, *God cultivated our courage.*

In August of 2015, we completed our eighth adoption home study. In October, the hormone supplements and injections began. On November 16, 2015, two of our remaining four embryos were thawed and transferred. God strengthened our resolve when we received a positive blood test just nine days later. God calmed our hearts when we learned that the one little life who had implanted was suddenly declared "non-viable" several weeks later. And God again increased our endurance as we waited until the twenty-first week of pregnancy for a natural miscarriage.

Determined to remain faithful to the very end, we made preparations to return one last time for our final two frozen embryos. They were successfully thawed and transferred on May 24, 2016. The first blood test confirmed another pregnancy; however, another miscarriage also took their lives shortly thereafter.

This time, God directed us down a path that ended much differently. This time, He never intended to add more children to our home. This time, He simply desired to develop our courage. Courage to overcome intense doubts and fears. Courage to follow. Courage to trust.

In the days that followed, we faced another major life decision regarding children. Throughout our fourteen years of marriage, the reproductive parts of my body had struggled to function properly. Pain and discomfort were often present. Unbalanced hormones produced a number of unusual side effects. My monthly periods were abnormally heavy and long.

However, upon the completion of a successful pregnancy and the end of all embryo transfer medications, every single side effect disappeared. It seemed that my body somehow reset itself and completely healed. At thirty-five years old, I now felt fairly confident that a biological child would result from any amount of effort.

But at the dawn of this new opportunity, *God taught us lessons about love.* He taught us that real *agape* love is always about what we give up and never about what we gain. He taught us that true love quickly lays aside any personal desires for the benefit of another. He taught us that sacrifice is essential and that self-denial is required.

As we contemplated the potential negative effects that a biological addition could have on our children, the decision was simple. We loved them enough to willingly give up anything of temporal insignificance. Anything that possibly communicated they were not enough. Anything that even hinted at dissatisfaction. Anything that provided opportunity for comparison among others. Anything that provided Satan additional ammo in his bag of destructive lies and deception.

With abundantly willing hearts that were filled with *agape* love, we scheduled a minor medical procedure that removed the possibility of genetic heirs. Our journey had finally come full circle. The prayers that once consumed us were but memories in the rearview mirror. As we reveled in the joy of all that God had accomplished, our dreams of long ago appeared so totally insignificant. So fleeting. So empty. So vain. They suddenly paled in comparison to the much richer blessings that accompanied a life devoted to following in the steps of the Miracle Man.

> *"This God—his way is perfect; the word of the LORD proves true; he is a shield for all those who take refuge in him"* (Psa. 18:30).

* * *

There is one final lesson that I have learned along the way. It is that sometimes God promotes better prayer. While the nature of God is abundantly patient and His heart is exceedingly kind, the Bible teaches that there is a wrong way to pray.

*"You ask and do not receive, because **you ask wrongly,** to spend it on your passions"* (Jas. 4:3—emphasis mine).

As I evaluate my own prayers, I realize just how selfish so many of them truly are. Prayers for my passions. Prayers for my comfort. Prayers for my ease.

As I listen each week to the requests of others, I see that I am not alone in this struggle. It seems that the vast majority of all the petitions I hear are for the sick to be healed, the bills to be paid, and the problems to be removed. For blessing in personal pursuits. For safety in all travel. For every unborn baby to be born healthy. For every child to succeed.

And God *wants* us to bring these things before His throne! He longs to be the source of our solutions and the healer of our pain! He delights to grant blessings and desires to give victory! But He also yearns to teach us about what really matters and to increase our understanding of acceptable prayer.

*"And this is the confidence that we have toward him, that if we ask anything **according to his will** he hears us"* (1 Jn. 5:14—emphasis mine).

This is the right way to pray! According to His will. It is not a tag that one adds to the conclusion of every prayer: "Please give me what I want . . . if it be Your will." But rather, it is a disciplined state of mind that requests things *known* to be God's will. It is often praying the very words of Scripture. It is always void of selfishness and pride. It always seeks man's eternal good and aims for God's ultimate glory.

Here are just a few examples of the many truths that are known to be God's will (all emphases mine):

1. **Personal sanctification**—*"For **this is the will of God**, your sanctification . . . "* (1 Thess. 4:3).

2. **Wisdom**—*"If any of you lacks wisdom, **let him ask God**, who gives generously to all without reproach, and it will be given him"* (Jas. 1:5).

3. **Strength**—*"**Seek** the Lord and his strength"* (1 Chron. 16:11a).

4. **Power to resist temptation**—*"**Pray** that you may not enter into temptation"* (Lk. 22:40).

5. **Salvation of others**—*"The Lord is . . . patient toward you, **not wishing that any should perish**, but that all should reach repentance"* (2 Pet. 3:9).

6. **Thanksgiving**—*"Give thanks in all circumstances; for **this is the will of God in Christ Jesus for you**"* (1 Thess. 5:18).

7. **Spiritual healing**—*"Therefore, confess your sins to one another and **pray** for one another, **that you may be healed**. The prayer of a righteous person has great power as it is working"* (Jas. 5:16).

8. **Confession**—*"I acknowledged my sin to you, and I did not cover my iniquity; I said, '**I will confess my transgressions** to the LORD,' and you forgave the iniquity of my sin. Selah"* (Psa. 32:5).

9. **Life of good works**—*"**For this is the will of God**, that by doing good you should put to silence the ignorance of foolish people"* (1 Pet. 2:15).

10. **Justice, kindness, humility**—*"He has told you, O man, what is good; and **what does the LORD require of you** but to do justice, and to love kindness, and to walk humbly with your God"* (Micah 6:8).

11. **Guidance**—*"Make me to know your ways, O LORD; **teach me your paths**"* (Psa. 25:4).

12. **Peace and rest**—*"**Come to me**, all who labor and are heavy laden, **and I will give you rest**. Take my yoke upon you, and learn from me, for I am gentle and lowly in heart, and you will find rest for your souls"* (Matt. 11:28-29).

This list is certainly not exhaustive! In fact, it barely scratches the surface of all we learn about the will of God throughout Scripture. But hopefully, it gives insight into this concept of praying according to His will.

Sometimes sickness, financial pressure, and relationship conflicts are part of God's perfect design. Our finite minds do not see the big picture as He does. We do not understand the purpose of pain. In moments of trial, we do not comprehend how they can possibly be good. And that is precisely why we must discipline ourselves to pray for what we know.

Now, a personal confession must be made here. I was first introduced to these lessons in the midst of my greatest earthly trials. While I begged God to open doors along our third adoption journey, He closed them left and right. Rejection. Fraud. Death. Powerlessness. Despair. Instead of the miracles I requested, He seemed to send only pain and heartache.

I wanted so desperately to believe that my Daddy God cared for the specifics of my life. I longed to communicate every detail to the One who never tired of listening. Above all, I needed to know that my personal desires somehow fit into His grand plan for the cosmos. That pouring out my heart before Him in prayer really mattered. Really made a difference. Really accomplished something.

Yet, during *this* time, I began to study what it means to pray according to God's will. During *this* time, He illumined the selfishness of my prayers. During *this* time, He challenged the despair that followed my earthly focus.

At first, a sadness accompanied such revelations. It seemed that God desired the details of my prayers be removed and replaced with a simple, "Whatever You want, Lord." It seemed that He desired an absence of disappointment in my trials. That I, like Paul, was expected to smile and worship while floating on flotsam adrift at sea. That if shipwrecks and imprisonments continued to come, I was supposed to rest in contentment, unaffected by such temporal discomforts.

However, deeper study brought great clarity to me. God wanted *both* my specifics *and* my submission! They were *not* mutually exclusive. A personal closeness to God accompanied the bearing of my every soul's desire to the One Who understood me above all others. A genuine comfort followed the communicating of my disappointment and loss. A trust in His sovereignty grew with the verbalizing of my submission to His plans over mine. And a confidence that my prayers *would be answered* came with the praying according to His will.

> *"And so, from the day we heard, we have not ceased to pray for you, asking that you may be filled with the knowledge of his will in all spiritual wisdom and understanding, so as to walk in a manner worthy of the Lord, fully pleasing to him, bearing fruit in every good work and increasing in the knowledge of God; being strengthened with all power, according to his glorious might, for all endurance and patience with joy; giving thanks to the Father who has qualified you to share in the inheritance of the saints in light"* (Col. 1:9–12).

The apostle Paul wrote these verses during his first, two-year imprisonment in Rome (ca. A.D. 60–62). While in bondage there, he also wrote the books of Ephesians and Philemon. Yet despite his chains and captivity, his letters bore little emphasis on his earthly discomforts. Rather than complaints regarding his unfair circumstances, Paul rejoiced in his sufferings (Col. 1:24) and gladly embraced the title, "prisoner of Christ." While Paul certainly desired deliverance and rescue, his prayers ascended far above such temporal trials and focused on the supremacy of Christ and the spiritual maturity of the saints.

The book of Colossians was written to the believers in Colossae after Paul received news that certain heretics dispersed false doctrines among them. Such teaching stressed a continued bondage to the Old Testament law and minimized the freedom offered at the cross. It promoted angel worship and the earthly perfection of an elite few. And it denied the very Deity of Jesus Christ.

These lies were diametrically opposed to everything Paul was imprisoned for teaching. While authorities sought to silence and stifle the truth, such false gospels were freely proclaimed. Discouragement and despair could have easily resulted from such circumstances. Yet in Colossians chapter one, Paul's prayer focused on the spiritual opportunities for growth that were presented *because* of them. He demonstrated perfectly how to pray for sanctification *in* trial as opposed to the mere removal *of* trial. Paul prayed that the Colossian believers would do the following:

1. **Be filled with the knowledge of God's will**—possess enlightenment from the Holy Spirit and have a complete filling of the inner man with a deep understanding of God's desires for every day decision-making[36]

2. **Walk in a manner worthy of the Lord**—Christ-like character that equals God's holy standards[37]

3. **Please God fully**—personal conduct that seeks to carry out God's wishes above man's wishes

4. **Bear fruit**—produce good works

5. **Increase in the knowledge of God**—deeper understanding of Who God is

6. **Receive supernatural strength**—spiritual vitality to overcome resistance

7. **Gain endurance**—*(hypomone)* constancy, steadfastness, and loyalty to faith despite even the greatest suffering[38]

8. **Grow in patience**—*(makrothymia)* gentleness and self-restraint toward others[39]

9. **Possess joy**—*(chara)* internal cheer and gladness[40]

10. **Proclaim gratitude**—external expressions of thanksgiving to God

This outline has greatly aided in organizing my ever-evolving prayers. It has lifted my focus upward and challenged my eternal perspective. It has highlighted the acceptable and provided a concrete example of prayer "according to God's will."

The paragraphs below attempt to demonstrate the practical outworking of such lessons in the prayers of twenty-first-century America. For the child who faces bullying at school. For the father who just lost his job. For the friend who is dying of cancer. They provide but a glimpse into my prayer closet as I draw near to my Father God and humbly commune with Him.

> Loving Jesus, I am gaining new understanding of sin's painful consequences. Its effects touch many and sting deeply. My heart aches as I watch my son suffer at the hand of school bullies, and I remember that Your tender heart aches, too. Please fill me with the wisdom to know when I should take action and when I should rest in Your justice. Help me to point my son to the sufferings of Jesus and the love that He showed to those nailing Him to the cross of Calvary. May my son gain understanding of Christ-like responses to the sins of others and desire to please You more than any earthly individual. May he learn to do good to his enemies and combat hatred with love. Give him power to overcome the temptation to retaliate and help him to remember the example of Christ on the cross. May the growth of his endurance and self-control result in joy and a clear conscience before You. And may he find daily reasons to thank You for the work You are doing in his life.

> Dear Father, You know the financial needs of this brother in Christ whom You dearly love. Please fill his heart with the perfect balance between trusting in You for daily provision and pursuing work to support his family. May Your Holy Spirit fill and enlighten him in the many decisions he now faces. In each job application and interview process, may he display the perfect character of Jesus Christ, and may gaining favor from potential employers never become more important than gaining Yours. Despite his circumstances, please protect him from self-pity and empower him to serve others. Grant steadfastness that clings to the Word of God, gentleness that overcomes pressure, and gladness that only

You can give. Even amid uncertainty, may he find daily reasons to give You thanks. And above all, may this trial result in a deeper understanding of Your limitless character.

God, I come boldly before Your throne on behalf of my dear friend who is battling cancer. I recognize that such intense suffering and pain were never part of Your original creation, and I look longingly toward the future when You will once again make all things new. Please replace her paralyzing fears with the peace that surpasses all understanding. Exchange her worries for an unwavering confidence that You are in sovereign control. Display Your magnificent power in her life, whether by physical healing or by spiritual sustaining. Give supernatural wisdom to the medical team as they make daily decisions regarding her care. Empower her to live out the character of Your Son as she walks this dark valley and to shine as a beacon of light among the hospital staff who walk with her. May she seek Your face daily and find strength to serve others even in the midst of her own pain. Grant the fortitude to overcome temptation and the constancy to keep going. May the perfect patience of Jesus Christ and the incomprehensible joy that only He can give be a powerful testimony to the doctors, nurses, and regular visitors who come before her. Fill her mouth with thanksgiving as You enlarge her understanding of Your goodness, sovereignty, power, and love.

What a transformation from my earthly prayers of long ago! My simple requests for the removal of suffering pale next to the wonders I now understand He can accomplish through such trials. To know His unfathomable peace at the brink of blindness far out-shadows any increase of sight. To experience His provision at the entrance to the impossible greatly outshines any path of ease. To learn His goodness at the hand of the hypocrite abundantly outweighs any absence of pain. To grow in grace infinitely outlasts any removal of dark valleys.

In the frantic and sleep-deprived first year with triplets, prayers for rest were replaced with prayers for patience. As they grew into a trio of toddlers who destroyed my furniture and defaced my carpet, I pleaded for contentment with my couches and satisfaction amid the stains. As every single monetary fee was multiplied by three, above and beyond the expenses of two older brothers, I requested freedom from my fears and investments in the eternal. As issues continued to arise with my eyesight, I sought wisdom in my weakness and confidence in His care. As I took on full-time employment once again and tried to balance the many pressures and responsibilities of this life, I begged for beauty in the busyness and solitude in my spirit. And as decisions regarding the future arose, I prayed for humility above honor and obedience above gain.

Many years ago, I came across an article entitled, *The Brotherhood of Sons* by Russell D. Moore. It told the story of how he and his wife, Maria, adopted two precious young boys from Russia. After the Russian courts finally matched them with children, they excitedly made the long trip overseas to meet Maxim and Sergei for the first time. But upon their arrival at the orphanage, they stated, "We almost vomited in reaction to the stench and the squalor of the place. The boys were in cribs in the dark, lying in their own waste."[41]

After several days of bonding with their soon-to-be sons, Russell and Maria were painfully forced to return to the U.S. alone to await the completion of their adoption paperwork. As they said their goodbyes at the orphanage, the boys collapsed in their cribs and convulsed with loud sobs. They desperately longed for the continued embrace of two strangers who had suddenly delivered hope to their dark world. In spite of the fact that these boys could not understand English yet, Russell placed his hands on their heads and simply said, "I will not leave you orphans; I will come to you" (Jn. 14:18).

Many days passed before Russell and Maria received the glorious phone call that the legal process was finally completed. They eagerly anticipated their return trip to Russia and the official adoption of their two new sons. Upon their return to the orphanage, they presented Maxim and Sergei with wildflowers and new clothes to travel home in. They hugged and laughed and excitedly chattered about the new life that awaited them in America.

When the papers were all signed, the new parents picked up their young boys and happily stepped outside the doors of the orphanage. But as they entered the sunshine, both boys instantly began to shake and cry. They reached their arms back toward the only place that they had ever called home and longed to return to its loneliness and despair. You see, they had never seen the sunlight or felt the wind in their faces. They had never heard the sound of birds in the trees or experienced the sensation of riding in a car. They were overwhelmed, confused, and frightened. Russell held Sergei in his arms and whispered in his ear, "That place is a pit! If only you knew what's waiting for you: a home with a mommy and daddy who love you, grandparents, and great-grandparents, and cousins, and McDonald's Happy Meals!" Surely, in time they would both become acclimated to their wonderful new life, but in those first moments of freedom they reached longingly back for the filth and hopelessness of the cold, dark orphanage.

Don't we all do this sometimes? God desires to give us abundant blessings of eternal value. Belonging. Love. Freedom. Security. Satisfaction. Peace. Power. Yet, so often we find comfort in our customs and happiness in our habits. We focus on what we must give up in order to experience all that God offers. We believe the deception of this world. We cling to our short-sighted view. We seek the fulfillment of our earthly passions that we conclude will satisfy our souls. And we pray that God would aid us in our efforts.

In the opening pages of this book, I stated the primary reason why this busy momma of five decided to take on the monumental task of recording her life story and the many lessons learned along the way. It was for them. It was written so that the gaze of these precious gifts would be directed to the Sovereign hand of God from the very beginning of their existence. It was designed to highlight His abundant goodness and to bear witness to the truth that a life devoted in humble service to Him will always be deemed worthwhile. It was intended to point them to Jesus. It was prompted by the words of Deuteronomy 4:9 as their encouragement to remember: "Only take care, and keep your soul diligently, lest you forget the things that your eyes have seen, and lest they depart from your heart all the days of your life. Make them known to your children and your children's children."

And so, I conclude this three-year venture with a prayer for them. Not a prayer for their health and happiness. Not a prayer for the simple joys that bring but moments of glee upon this earth. But rather, it is a prayer for their eternal good and for the glory of an incomprehensible God.

> Dear kind and gracious Heavenly Father, I thank You from the bottom of my heart for giving my barren womb a joyous home and filling it with exceeding abundance far beyond my simple dreams of long ago. I thank You for the trials of my life that drive me to my knees and draw me closer to the loving heart of Jesus. And I thank You for the glimpses of Your unfathomable character that I glean along the way.
>
> Please accomplish a similar work in the lives of my children. First and foremost, may Griffen, Rhys, Taerik, Drake, and Keira each come to a saving knowledge of the Lord Jesus Christ. May they each recognize their inherent sinfulness and their total inability to save themselves from the eternal punishment that they deserve. Guide them to the cross of Calvary and the abundant life of freedom that it offers. Rescue them from the dark walls of their "orphanage" and carry them into the sunshine of Your Son.
>
> Help them to grow in the grace and knowledge of the Lord Jesus Christ. Help them to recognize Your supernatural hand of guidance in placing them in our family. May they understand Your tender mercies in removing them from a helpless and desperate place. Empower them to be still and know that You are God rather than to clamor for the pieces of their past that You withhold. May they embrace the path of Your choosing and reject the lies of this world—lies that move their focus away from Your goodness. Help them to find their sense of belonging and acceptance in Christ

alone, and may any scars they bear be proud reminders of Your love and watch care over them.

Along their life journey, fill them with the knowledge of Your will and develop their spiritual wisdom. Point their feet in the direction that pleases You and overflow their harvest with good fruit. Cultivate their courage. Heighten their holiness. Increase their endurance. Promote their patience. Obtain their obedience. Grow their gratitude.

Lastly, I pray that my life would bear witness to the truth that humble submission to a holy God is worth any sacrifice He requires. May they understand that valleys are valuable. That waiting brings wisdom. That risks are rewarding. That pain is profitable. That heartache grows holiness. That miracles still happen. And may they clearly realize that they are each the joyous conclusion of their mother's very long path to answered prayer.

ON PATHS TO ANSWERED PRAYER

By Heidi Fuller

Have you ever wondered if your prayers are really heard?
Why is your path so lonely if God listens to each word?
When answers seem so distant through years of faithful pleas,
Still your Guide is right beside you each moment on your knees.

In the wilderness He's working;
In the dark, do not despair.
In the storms, He's sanctifying;
In the thunder, He is there.
Out of valleys, He gives victories;
Out of chaos, comes a calm.
Out of testing, He brings triumph;
Out of sorrow comes a song.

At last the destination through weary eye appears;
But rather than rejoicing, prayer's journey ends in tears.
When answers seem so different from anything you planned,
Trust your Sovereign Father and hold His loving hand.

Find power in His promise,
Though at times not understood.
As you love the God Who leads you,
He will guide your path to good.
Though there's weeping in the waiting,
In the morning joy is there.
Learn to trust Him as you travel
On the paths to answered prayer.[42]

ENDNOTES

1. John MacArthur, "The Gift of Peace," *Grace To You,* https://www.gty.org/library/articles/P21/the-gift-of-peace (accessed October 6, 2018).

2. Ibid.

3. Heidi Fuller, *Give Me Eyes That See,* Forever Be Sure, 2012, https://foreverbesure.com/product/give-me-eyes-that-see/.

4. Heidi Fuller, *You Numbered All My Days,* Forever Be Sure, 2007, https://foreverbesure.com/product/you-numbered-all-my-days/.

5. John Walvoord and Roy Zuck, *The Bible Knowledge Commentary* (Dallas, TX: Dallas Theological Seminary: 1989).

6. Bodie Hodge, "How Long Did It Take For Noah To Build The Ark?," Answers In Genesis, https://answersingenesis.org/bible-timeline/how-long-did-it-take-for-noah-to-build-the-ark/ (accessed October 7, 2018).

7. Heidi Fuller, *The Price He Paid For Me,* Forever Be Sure, 2012. https://foreverbesure.com/product/the-price-he-paid-for-me/.

8. Blue Letter Bible, *s.v. "arkeo,"* accessed October 7, 2018, https://www.blueletterbible.org/lang/lexicon/lexicon.cfm?Strongs=G714&t=KJV.

9. James Strong, *s.v.* "satisfy," *Strong's Expanded Exhaustive Concordance of the Bible* (Nashville: Thomas Nelson, 2010).

10. Paul David Tripp, *A Quest For More: Living for Something Bigger Than You* (Greensboro, NC: New Growth Press, 2013).

11. Ibid.

12. Ibid.

13. Ibid.

14. Ibid.

15. Blue Letter Bible, *s.v.* "hypomone," accessed October 6, 2018, https://www.blueletterbible.org/lang/lexicon/lexicon.cfm?Strongs=G5281&t=KJV.

16. Rodney Griffin, "'I Choose' by Rodney Griffin" *Joy in my Journey,* https://joyinmyjourney.wordpress.com/2012/01/25/i-choose-by-rodney-griffin/ (accessed October 7, 2018).

17. C.H. Spurgeon, "Samuel, An Example of Intercession No. 1537," *Bible.org.* https://bible.org/seriespage/9-samuel-example-intercession-no-1537 (accessed September 8, 2018).

18. Ibid.

19. Ibid.

20. Ibid.

21. David Ward, "I'll Never Forsake You," *Thousand Tongues,* http://www.thousandtongues.org/songs/modernhymns/ill-never-forsake-you (accessed October 7, 2018).

22. Rodney Griffin, "Greater Vision–It Pays To Pray," *NameThatHymn.com,* https://namethathymn.com/hymn-lyrics/viewtopic.php?t=12507   (accessed October 7, 2018).

23. Greater Vision, "I've Been To The Bottom," YouTube video, Duration 3:32, Posted April 7, 2016, https://www.youtube.com/watch?v=Rc5A1105ALU.

24. Remah Kamel, "Assisted Reproductive Technology after the birth of Louise Brown," Omicsonline.org. https://www.omicsonline.org/assisted-repro-ductive-technology-after-the-birth-of-louise-brown-2161-0932.1000156.php?aid=16043 (accessed September 15, 2018).

25. Michaeleen Doucleff, "IVF Baby Boom: Births From Fertility Procedures Hit   New   High,"   NPR.org,   https://www.npr.org/sections/health-shots/2014/02/18/279035110/ivf-baby-boom-births-from-fertility-proce-dure-hit-new-high (accessed September 15, 2018).

26. Jasmine Taylor-Coleman, "The Americans who 'adopt' other people's embryos," BBC.com. https://www.bbc.com/news/magazine-36450328 (accessed September 15, 2018).

27. Andrew Hough, "1.7 million human embryos created for ivf thrown away,"   Telegraph.co.uk.   https://www.telegraph.co.uk/news/health/news/9772233/1.7-million-human-embryos-created-for-IVF-thrown-away.html (accessed September 15, 2018).

28. "A look at the History of Adoption and Embryo Adoption," Embryoadoption.org.   https://www.embryoadoption.org/2012/06/a-look-at-the-history-of-adoption-and-embryo-adoption/ (accessed September 15, 2018).

29. Rob Blackhurst, "The pro-lifers adopting 'spare' embryos created dur-ing   ivf,"   Telegraph.co.uk.   https://www.telegraph.co.uk/news/health/news/10353338/The-pro-lifers-adopting-spare-embryos-created-during-IVF.html (accessed September 15, 2018).

30. "About NEDC," Embryodonation.org, https://www.embryodonation. org/about/ (accessed September 15, 2018).

31. "Adoption FAQs," Embryodonation.org. https://www.embryodonation. org/adoption/ (accessed September 22, 2018).

32. Mark Mellinger (NEDC Marketing and Development Director), Interviewed by Heidi Fuller via email, September 23, 2018.

33. Heidi Fuller, *I Know, Forever Be Sure, 2013.* https://foreverbesure.com/ product/i-know/.

34. Heidi Fuller, "Ephesians 3:20-21," Somuchmore2014@blogspot.com, http://somuchmore2014.blogspot.com/2013/11/ephesians-320-21.html, November 7, 2013.

35. Heidi Fuller, *So Much More,* Forever Be Sure, 2012. https://foreverbesure. com/product/so-much-more/.

36. John Walvoord and Roy Zuck, *The Bible Knowledge Commentary* (Dallas, TX: Dallas Theological Seminary: 2002).

37. Ibid.

38. Blue Letter Bible, *s.v. "hypomone,"* accessed October 6, 2018, https://www. blueletterbible.org/lang/lexicon/lexicon.cfm?Strongs=G5281&t=KJV.

39. Blue Letter Bible, *s.v. "makrothymia,"* accessed October 6, 2018, https:// www.blueletterbible.org/lang/lexicon/lexicon.cfm?Strongs=G3115&t=KJV.

40. Blue Letter Bible, *s.v. "chara,"* accessed October 6, 2018, https://www. blueletterbible.org/lang/lexicon/lexicon.cfm?Strongs=G5479&t=KJV.

41. Russell D. Moore, "The Brotherhood of Sons," *Touchstone,* https://www.touchstonemag.com/archives/article.php?id=20-04-026-f (accessed October 7, 2018).

42. Heidi Fuller, *On Paths to Answered Prayer.* Shawnee Press, 2016. https://www.shawneepress.com/product/viewproduct.action?itemid=35031277&lid=40&subsiteid=204&whatsnew=365&subsiteid=204&.

BIBLIOGRAPHY

Blue Letter Bible. Accessed October 07, 2018. https://www.blueletterbible.org/lang/lexicon/lexicon.cfm?Strongs=G714&t=KJV.

Blackhurst, Rob. "The Pro-lifers Adopting 'spare' Embryos Created during IVF." *The Telegraph*. Accessed October 07, 2018. https://www.telegraph.co.uk/news/health/news/10353338/The-pro-lifers-adopting-spare-embryos-created-during-IVF.html.

Doucleff, Michaeleen. "IVF Baby Boom: Births From Fertility Procedures Hit New High." *NPR*. Accessed October 07, 2018. https://www.npr.org/sections/health-shots/2014/02/18/279035110/ivf-baby-boom-births-from-fertility-procedure-hit-new-high.

Fuller, Heidi. "Ephesians 3:20-21." So Much More . . . Accessed October 07, 2018. http://somuchmore2014.blogspot.com/2013/11/ephesians-320-21.html.

Hodge, Bodie. "How Long Did It Take for Noah to Build the Ark?" Answers in Genesis. Accessed October 07, 2018. https://answersingenesis.org/bible-timeline/how-long-did-it-take-for-noah-to-build-the-ark/.

Hough, Andrew. "1.7 Million Human Embryos Created for IVF Thrown Away." *The Telegraph*. Accessed October 07, 2018. https://www.telegraph.co.uk/news/health/news/9772233/1.7-million-human-embryos-created-for-IVF-thrown-away.html.

Kamel, Remah MA. "Assisted Reproductive Technology after the Birth of Louise Brown." OMICS International. Accessed October 07, 2018. https://www.omicsonline.org/assisted-reproductive-technology-after-the-birth-of-louise-brown-2161-0932.1000156.php?aid=16043.

MacArthur, John. "The Gift of Peace." *Grace to You*. Accessed October 07, 2018. https://www.gty.org/library/articles/P21/the-gift-of-peace.

Mellinger, Mark. E-mail interview by author. September 23, 2018.

Moore, Russell D. "The Brotherhood of Sons." *Touchstone: A Journal of Mere Christianity*. Accessed October 07, 2018. https://www.touchstonemag.com/archives/article.php?id=20-04-026-f.

NEDC. "About The National Embryo Donation Center." NEDC. Accessed October 07, 2018. https://www.embryodonation.org/about/.

Nightlight Christian Adoptions. "A Look at the History of Adoption and Embryo Adoption." Embryo Adoption Awareness Center. Accessed October 07, 2018. https://www.embryoadoption.org/2012/06/a-look-at-the-history-of-adoption-and-embryo-adoption/.

Spurgeon, C. H. "Samuel, An Example of Intercession No. 1537." Bible.org. Accessed October 07, 2018. https://bible.org/seriespage/9-samuel-example-intercession-no-1537.

Strong, James. *The New Strongs Expanded Exhaustive Concordance of the Bible* (Nashville: Thomas Nelson, 2010).

Taylor-Coleman, Jasmine. "The Americans Who 'adopt' Other People's Embryos." *BBC News*. Accessed October 07, 2018. https://www.bbc.com/news/magazine-36450328.

Tripp, Paul David. *Quest for More: Living for Something Bigger than You* (Place of Publication Not Identified: New Growth Press, 2013).

NEDC. "Understanding Embryo Adoption." NEDC. Accessed October 07, 2018. https://www.embryodonation.org/adoption/.

Walvoord, John F., and Roy B. Zuck. *Bible Knowledge Commentary*. Dallas, TX: CDWord Library, 1989.

DISCOGRAPHY

"Forever Be Sure." http://www.foreverbesure.com/. Accessed October 7, 2018.

Fuller, Heidi. "Give Me Eyes That See." *Forever Be Sure*. 2012. https://forever-besure.com/product/give-me-eyes-that-see/. Accessed October 07, 2018.

Fuller, Heidi. "I Know." *Forever Be Sure*, 2013. https://foreverbesure.com/product/i-know/. Accessed October 7, 2018.

Fuller, Heidi. "The Price He Paid for Me." *Forever Be Sure*, 2012. https://forever-besure.com/product/the-price-he-paid-for-me/. Accessed October 07, 2018.

Fuller, Heidi. "On Paths to Answered Prayer." *Shawnee Press*, 2016. https://www.shawneepress.com/product/viewproduct.action?itemid=35031277&lid=40&subsiteid=204&whatsnew=365&subsiteid=204&. Accessed October 07, 2018.

Fuller, Heidi. "So Much More." *Forever Be Sure*, 2012. https://foreverbesure.com/product/so-much-more/. Accessed October 07, 2018.

Fuller, Heidi. "You Numbered All My Days." *Forever Be Sure*, 2007. https://foreverbesure.com/product/you-numbered-all-my-days/. Accessed October 07, 2018.

Greater Vision. "I've Been to The Bottom." YouTube video, Duration 3:32, Posted April 7, 2016, https://www.youtube.com/watch?v=Rc5A1105ALU. Accessed October 07, 2018.

Griffin, Rodney. "I Choose." *Joy in My Journey.* https://joyinmyjourney.word-press.com/2012/01/25/i-choose-by-rodney-griffin/. Accessed October 7, 2018.

Griffin, Rodney. "It Pays To Pray." *NameThatHymn.com.* https://nametha-thymn.com/hymn-lyrics/viewtopic.php?t=12507. Accessed October 7, 2018.

Ward, David. "I'll Never Forsake You," *Thousand Tongues.* http://www.thou-sandtongues.org/songs/modernhymns/ill-never-forsake-you.   Accessed October 7, 2018.

For more information about

Heidi Fuller
and
Paths to Answered Prayer
please visit:

www.somuchmore2014.blogspot.com
www.facebook.com/hfullerkansas
hfullerkansas@hotmail.com

For more information about
AMBASSADOR INTERNATIONAL
please visit:

www.ambassador-international.com
@AmbassadorIntl
www.facebook.com/AmbassadorIntl

If you enjoyed this book, please consider leaving us a review on
Amazon, Goodreads, or our website.

Made in the
USA
Columbia, SC